# THE
# FIO
# MINDSET

FIO PRESS 26 Wadleigh Lane South Berwick, ME 03908

First Edition 2025

ISBN 979-8-9930630-0-3 (Hardcover)

ISBN 979-8-9930630-1-0 (Paperback)

ISBN 979-8-9930630-3-4 (eBook)

Library of Congress Control Number: 2025925323 Library of Congress Cataloging-in-Publication Data is available.

The FIO Loop™, The FIO Mindset™, and Launching Beliefs™ are trademarks of Rachel Martin.

*To Brad – you are my biggest cheerleader and help me to become the best version of myself. Thank you for your decades of support, encouragement and love.*

*To my children – Olivia, Ethan, and Hazel – so you never have to wonder who I was.*

# CONTENTS

## PART III: ACHIEVE: *Becoming Someone Who Figures Things Out*

# About the Author

Rachel Martin is a lifelong community builder, endurance event producer, personal growth junkie, and creator of *The FIO Mindset* — a transformational framework helping people move from hesitation to bold, confident action.

She's not a therapist or psychologist. She's a stay-at-home mom turned movement maker. A woman who figured it out by doing — one bold move and google search at a time.

Over the past two decades, Rachel has led some of the most beloved endurance events in New England, raised nearly a million dollars combined for local causes, and created ripple effects that have reached from her hometown in Southern Maine to dream-chasers across the country. She's the founder of **Forward Motion Events**, owner of **The Pumpkinman Triathlon & Running Festival**, and the heart behind **Rick's Run 5k**, a 5K honoring her late father's legacy.

Rachel is living proof that you don't need a fancy degree or perfect plan to build a life of meaning — you just need the courage to start and the belief that you'll figure it out as you go.

She's married to her high school sweetheart, Brad, and together they've raised three amazing children — Olivia, Ethan, and Hazel, and together are now welcoming their next chapter as grandparents to twin girls. Rachel's life is powered by purpose, dark chocolate, messy action, and a deep belief in what's possible.

She FIO'd this book into existence…She believes in people more than they often believe in themselves and, if you're holding this book, she believes in you.

# FOREWARD

There are moments in life when you witness someone transform an idea into a movement, and when you do, you know you're watching something extraordinary unfold. For me, that someone has always been Rachel.

I've had the privilege of walking beside Rachel along every chapter of her journey. As her husband, her biggest supporter, and as someone who continues to learn from her every single day. When I stop to examine what she has accomplished throughout her lifetime, I see a story of courage, creativity, and unwavering commitment to making a difference. *The FIO Mindset* is the essence of that story. It's not just a book; it's a philosophy forged in real-world challenges and triumphs, and it's one that can help you change the way you live, lead, and love.

---

Why This Book Matters

We live in a world that moves fast—sometimes too fast. Distractions are everywhere, uncertainty is constant, and the pressure to "do more" is relentless. In the midst of that chaos, it's easy to lose sight of what truly matters. Rachel wrote this book because she knows what it feels like to stand in the middle of it all and she has mastered how to find calm, clarity, and purpose within it.

*The FIO Mindset*—Figure It Out—is not a slogan. It's a way of thinking and living that empowers you to take control of your choices, your time, and your impact. It's about embracing challenges with confidence, solving problems creatively, and refusing to be paralyzed by uncertainty. Rachel's mantra, one which she often shares on her podcast, captures it best: ***"You*** *don't need more time. You just need to figure it out.*" That's the heartbeat of this book.

---

Rachel's Journey: Creating Start and Finish Lines

When I think about Rachel's entrepreneurial journey, the images that come to mind are start and finish lines. Throughout the years and through all of her endeavors, Rachel has created thousands of them, both literally and symbolically. She has built spaces which allow people to begin something new, push through challenges, and cross a line that represents transformation. These athletic events aren't just races; they're experiences that remind people of what's possible when they commit, persevere, and simply Figure It Out.

Forward Motion Events is more than a business—it's a movement. It's about giving people the courage to start and the strength to finish. Rachel has always believed that the finish line isn't the end, rather it's proof that you can do hard things. And the start line? That is where the magic and possibility begin. This philosophy guides everything she does, and it's why Forward Motion Events has become a beacon for community, resilience, and joy.

Rachel's other ventures including real estate investments, opening a yoga studio, and all of her volunteerism are further examples of her ability to see opportunity and act. Yet it is through Forward Motion Events, where her heart beats loudest. Here is where she helps people discover their own strength.

---

## Themes That Define Her Work

If you've listened to Rachel's podcast, you know her voice is full of energy and conviction. She talks about pivoting as a strength, not a weakness. She reminds us that clarity comes through action, not waiting for perfect conditions. One of my favorite themes from her show is the Flip It Method: *Name it, Claim it, Flip it.* When fear shows up, Rachel teaches us to flip it into fuel. That's the essence of *The FIO Mindset*—turning obstacles into opportunities.

Resilience and adaptability: Rachel shares stories of race days when storms threatened to cancel events, and how quick thinking and resourcefulness saved the day. She calls this "adaptive expertise"—doing what you can with what you have, right now. That is what Figure It Out looks like in action.

Community: It is what lies at the heart of Rachel's events—The Pumpkinman Triathlon and Running Festival, Rick's Run 5K, Luna Run. These aren't just athletic competitions, rather they are celebrations of connection, inclusivity, and joy. They raise funds for causes, bring people together, and create memories that last a lifetime. Her podcast echoes this theme: success is not solitary; it's shared.

---

## Family: Her Greatest Achievement

Of all her accomplishments, the one that fills me with the deepest pride is the life we've built together and the family we continue to raise. Rachel is the mother of our three incredible children, and she has poured into them the same principles you'll find in this book: Figure things out, embrace challenges, and take ownership of your choices. She has created a home that is warm, vibrant, and full of love—a place where curiosity is encouraged, kindness is celebrated, and dreams are nurtured.

Rachel's ability to balance the demands of leadership with the joys of motherhood is nothing short of inspiring. She has shown our children and everyone around her—that success is not about sacrificing what matters most; it's about integrating your values into every part of your life.

## The FIO Mindset: A Framework for Life

the essence of figure it out is resilience and resourcefulness. It's about asking, "How can I solve this?" instead of saying, "I can't." It's about leaning into challenges with confidence and creativity. Rachel teaches us that when you adopt the FIO Mindset, you stop waiting for perfect conditions and start creating solutions. This mindset can be applied to every aspect of your life: In business, in relationships, as well as in personal growth. It's a universal tool for living with clarity and purpose.

## A Personal Reflection

As her husband, I've had a front-row seat to Rachel's journey. I've seen her wrestle with doubts, navigate setbacks, and rise stronger every time. I've watched her turn obstacles into stepping stones and transform challenges into opportunities. I've seen the courage it takes to lead with conviction in a world that often rewards conformity. And I've seen the joy that comes from knowing you've made a difference.

Rachel often says that mindset is the multiplier. Skills matter, strategies matter—but mindset amplifies them all. I couldn't agree more. In my own leadership journey (leading a billion-dollar company), I've seen how the right mindset can unlock potential and propel progress. This book gives you that mindset. It's a gift, and I'm honored to introduce it to you.

A Call to Action

As you read *The FIO Mindset*, I encourage you to do more than absorb information. Engage with it. Reflect on it. Apply it. This is not a passive concept; it's a call to action. It invites you to examine your patterns, challenge your assumptions, and elevate your game. It's about becoming the architect of your own destiny.

---

Closing Thoughts

So, whether you're a CEO steering a global enterprise, an entrepreneur building a dream, or an individual seeking clarity in a chaotic world, *The FIO Mindset* will equip you to embrace challenges, solve problems, and figure it out—every time. And in doing so, you'll not only achieve success—you'll define it on your own terms.

Enjoy the journey.

Brad Martin
CEO, Author, Husband, Partner, and Biggest Fan of Rachel Martin

"There are seven days in the week and someday isn't one of them." —anonymous

# INTRODUCTION

There's a lie you've been telling yourself.

Maybe it sounds like: "I'm not ready yet." Or "I need more time." Or "I'll do it when I'm more prepared."

You think this is wisdom. You think this is being responsible.

But it's the exact thing keeping you stuck.

You're suffering from "someday-itis"—that chronic condition where everything important gets scheduled for a day that doesn't exist:

- "Someday I'll be ready."
- "Someday I'll have the perfect plan."
- "Someday I'll know enough."
- "Someday I'll feel confident."

Every day you wait, you're not getting more prepared.

**You are simply getting better at waiting.**

You are strengthening neural pathways that make hesitation your default. You're becoming someone who doesn't take action—not because you can't, but because you've trained yourself not to.

The "someday-itis" is spreading—from your dreams to your daily life, from this year's goals to next year's excuses. Left untreated, it becomes terminal. Not to your life, but to your dreams.

And here's the truth most people don't want to hear: You are not lazy. You're just wired for safety. (Which is kind of sweet when you think about it. Your brain loves you so much it's trying to protect you from everything, including your own greatness.)

But "someday-itis" isn't protecting you. It's killing your potential one postponement at a time.

The cure? Three letters that will change everything:

FIO.

"The only impossible journey is the one you never begin."

—Tony Robbins

# The Moment Everything Changed

I stood at the starting line of the Boston Marathon in April 2007 with no business being there.

I'd never run a race. Not a 5K. Not even the local turkey trot on Thanksgiving morning. Nothing. THE Boston Marathon, the pinnacle race that runners train years to qualify for, was literally my first organized run.

Who does that?

Oh, and I'd just gotten over bronchitis. Because apparently, I like to make things interesting.

Rewind four months earlier. My friend Mike had asked if I wanted to join his sister's charity team, just raise $3,500. "Easy peasy," I thought.

I hesitated for about three seconds.

Part of me knew this was completely bonkers. But something deeper, something I couldn't quite name, whispered that I could figure it out. So I said yes. Because why not add "marathon runner" to my list of things I'm wildly unqualified for?

Now here I was at the starting line, and every rational voice in my head was having a full-blown meltdown: "What are you doing? You don't belong here. You're going to die. They're going to have to carry you off in one of those golf carts of shame."

But that same tiny whisper from January was still there—maybe 2% of my brain—saying: "But what if you don't die? What if you just...figure it out?"

So I had an escape plan if I needed it: Mile 8. That's where Brad and the kids would be cheering. If I needed to bail, that was my out. I could fake a dramatic injury, limp over to them, and we could all go get pancakes. But after mile 8? I knew the truth:

**The only way out is through.**

(I use that phrase all the time now. In business. In life. When I'm assembling IKEA furniture. Sometimes the only exit strategy is to keep going.)

Twenty-six point two miles later, I crossed that finish line—still alive, still vertical (mostly), and with a truth that would change everything:

**There isn't anything I can't do.**

And the same applies to you. Yeah, you. Reading this right now, probably thinking "but she doesn't know my situation." You're right. I don't. But I know fear. I know doubt. And I know what happens when you decide to FIO anyway.

## The Language I'd Been Missing

For years before and after the Boston Marathon, I kept doing impossible things.

Finding rides to sports when I was nine years old so I could play? **Figured it out.**

Creating what would become an annual end-of-school-year event at my kids' school? **Figured it out.**

Buying a building and running a yoga studio? **Figured it out.**

Creating Rick's Run at midnight while ugly-crying through American Sniper? **Figured it out.**

Helping to create and nurture a sister city between South Berwick, Maine and Tuskegee, Alabama? **Figured it out.**

Getting to the final auditions for TEDx not one or two times, but three times? Still **figuring it out.** (By the way, I am still figuring it out...maybe the fourth time will be the charm!)

Buying a triathlon? **Figured it out.**

Pitching Jesse Itzler—the entrepreneur who sold Marquis Jets to Warren Buffett, ZICO Coconut Water to Coca-Cola, co-owns the Atlanta Hawks, and creates endurance events that push humans to their limits: convincing him it was a great idea to have an inaugural public "Hell on the Hill" event back-to-back with Pumpkinman in South Berwick? **Figured it out.**

Every seemingly impossible thing? **I. Figured. It. Out.**

I was always figuring it out, but never giving a name to this thing I was doing.

Then in 2020, I found myself in a Zoom planning meeting for one of the most grueling endurance races on the planet: Race Across America (RAAM).

The Race Across America is not your average endurance event—it's an *ultramarathon on wheels,* stretching from Oceanside, California, to Annapolis, Maryland. Riders face over **170,000 feet of vertical climbing**, scorching desert heat, mountain storms, pitch-black roads at 3 AM, and sleep deprivation so intense it feels like a science experiment in human willpower.

This isn't a "race" in the traditional sense. It's a test of *teamwork, grit, navigation, survival strategy,* and *mental durability.* Crews chase the riders in RVs, leapfrogging through the night, fueled by caffeine, adrenaline, and spreadsheets. Communication is often via walkie-talkies and shouted commands. Navigators ride shotgun with maps taped to dashboards, praying they don't miss a turn. You don't just do RAAM. You *become* RAAM, and it transforms you.

RAAM pushes people—athletes and crew alike—to the edge of what's humanly possible. You witness people break down, then build themselves back stronger in the span of hours. It's where you learn that courage is contagious. That the darkest moments are often followed by the most triumphant. Members of our team who are members of our military have dubbed it the closest experience civilians can get to a military operation. Brutally close quarters, little sleep, figuring things out in the moment and while all being driven by the mission.

It's one of the most *brutal, beautiful, and bonding* experiences in the endurance world. I've been fortunate enough (or crazy enough depending on who I am talking to) to have participated in this race three times.

Back to the zoom meeting- not only was I attending this as a crew member, but also as a co-crew chief in charge of the night shift. All without ever having experienced the race. The Zoom room buzzed with veteran racers who knew exactly how brutal, chaotic, and unpredictable this race would be. I was brand new. And I was all in.

Someone asked about logistics. About what happens when things go wrong in the middle of nowhere at 3 AM. About contingency plans and backup strategies.

And someone on the team said something that stopped me cold:

**"We'll just FIO."**

**Figure. It. Out.**

**Three letters. Three words. It was at this moment everything clicked.**

This is what I'd been doing my entire life. I'd been living this way for decades, but I'd never had language for it. That willingness to start before I was ready, to trust myself to handle whatever came next, to move despite fear—now it had a name: **FIO.**

And once I had the language, everything changed. Because I could teach it. I could share it. I could show other people that this wasn't some special gift—it was a choice. A system. A mindset. A way of not wanting to take life for granted.

## Creating Finish Lines, Crossing Fear Lines

For those who don't know me...I create finish lines for people. But between you and me?

**What I really create are permission slips for transformation.**

After watching thousands of athletes cross fear lines, after living the FIO way before I even knew what to call it, I discovered the pattern. A three-step loop that I had been living over and over that **transforms overthinkers into action-takers.**

This book is my gift to you: Twenty-two years of lessons compressed into eight chapters. Decades of hesitation-breaking discoveries delivered in days.

You don't have to wait as long as I did to understand this. You don't have to lose what I lost to gain urgency. You don't have to spend years suffering from "someday-itis" when you can start figuring it out today.

I've watched thousands of people at starting lines, that beautiful moment when excitement and terror have a baby and it looks like nervous energy. They all have that same look in their eyes:

*Do I belong here? Did I accidentally sign up for the wrong thing? Is it too late to pretend I have the flu?*

YES, you belong here. NO, you didn't sign up wrong. And YES, it's too late to fake the flu—we can see you, you look fine.

Here's what I've learned from watching all those terrified faces at starting lines: Every single person thinks they're the only one who doesn't belong. Guess what? Every single person is wrong.

**They ALL belong.**

Fear doesn't show up randomly. It shows up at the exact boundary between who you are now and who you're becoming. That boundary? I like to call it your Fear Line.

Most people see that line and back away. They think fear means "stop" or "danger" or "you're not meant to do this."

*But fear is just a marker.* It's showing you where your next level is, where your growth lives. Where the version of you that you dream about is waiting.

The real question isn't "Am I scared?" Of course you are. The real question is: **Why not you?**

Why shouldn't you be the one who crosses that line?

That conversation you're avoiding? **Fear Line-** Cross it.

That business keeping you up at night? **Fear Line-** Build it.

That race you bookmarked seventeen times? **Fear Line-** Register, (seriously, your browser history is judging you.)

That resignation letter saved in your drafts folder since 2021? That 'I love you' you haven't said? That apology gathering dust in your chest?

**Fear Lines. All of them.**

Let me guess yours.

It's that thing you thought about three times while reading this page. The one making your stomach tighten right now.

Yeah, that one.

That life you keep saying "someday?" It's right there, waiting. Probably tapping its foot by now.

Every day you stand at that line without crossing it, you're practicing being someone who doesn't. You are riddled with ""someday-itis"."

"Someday-itis"- that chronic condition where everything important gets scheduled for a day that doesn't exist.

## Time Is Not Unlimited

I was six when my mom was killed in a car accident. Lost my dad 30 years later.

Those losses taught me something: We don't get unlimited time. We don't get do-overs. We only get right now.

Read that again. **We. Only. Get. Right. Now.** Not tomorrow. Not after the promotion. Now.

I could have let that make me bitter. Instead, it gave me clarity about what actually matters.

My biggest fear isn't failure. It's getting to the end of my life with regrets. It's looking back and seeing all the Fear Lines I didn't cross, all the chances I didn't take, all the times I chose safe over alive.

That fear—the fear of regret—drives everything I do. Every race I create, every starting line I stand at, every person I push to FIO.

I tell you this because I want you to get to your rocking chair at the end of your life and smile at how fully you lived, not ache for what you didn't try.

You might have heard the saying, where your focus goes, energy flows. I choose to focus on what's possible instead of what's been lost. Not because I'm naturally optimistic, but because I learned early that wallowing doesn't change anything. Action does.

This truth isn't meant to scare you. It's actually meant to wake you up. To help you realize that waiting for "ready" is like waiting for your junk drawer to organize itself. It's not happening. Trust me, I've been waiting 18 years for mine to get its act together.

28

The alternative—getting to the end with a list of "what ifs" and "if onlys"—that's the real tragedy.

The time is going to pass anyway, so you might as well FIO.

## What Is The FIO Mindset?

FIO stands for Figure It Out—but it's more than an acronym.

A mindset is the lens through which you see the world. It's your internal operating system—your thoughts, your beliefs, assumptions, and inner dialogue. They all quietly dictate what you believe is possible, how you respond to challenges, whether you wait or move.

Change your mindset, change your outcomes, change your life. You also change how you see the world and your role in it.

The FIO Mindset goes beyond belief. It's not just something you think—it's something you become.

There is a gap between believing and doing. That's where dreams go to take really long naps. That's where regrets are born. The FIO Mindset bridges that gap. It's not just believing you can learn—it's starting before you've YouTubed every possible tutorial. It's choosing optimism about what's possible while accepting you might face-plant a few times, and that is ok. It's trusting yourself to figure it out along the way.

It's the difference between nodding at TED talks and actually doing the thing. Between saving inspiring posts and actually signing up for your own adventure. Between being the person who says "I've always wanted to do that" and the person who says "So I signed up yesterday." It's a simple three-step loop that moves you from 'I can't' to 'I did':

F - Face the Fear & Flip It

I - Identify One Action

O - Observe, Optimize & Celebrate

But here's the thing—this loop only works if you understand why you're not using it already. It only works when you realize that everything comes down to one simple formula:

**Thoughts→ Beliefs → Mindset → Action**

Change your thoughts, Change your beliefs, Change your mindset, Change your actions:

**Change your life.**

There are 3 Paths you can be on. Most people are stuck on Path 1 (I can't) or Path 2 (I'm not ready). This book will put you on Path 3 (I'll figure it out).

And once you're on Path 3, the FIO Loop keeps you there.

## But I'm Really Not Ready

Cool. Join the club.

We meet at every starting line, every first day, every big decision. We have jackets. (Okay, we don't have jackets, but we should).

Nobody feels ready. The difference between the people who do the thing and the ones who don't?

The doers know that "ready" is a myth—like inbox zero or just one more episode. They know that regret weighs more than failure ever will.

So if you're thinking: "But I'm really not ready..."

What if that's not a stop sign—but a signal? What if the thing that scares you most is actually pointing to your next step? What if waiting is the only thing you'll actually regret?

(Spoiler: It is.)

## Who You'll Become

You didn't pick up this book because you wanted more information. You picked it up because something inside you is done waiting.

This isn't just a mindset you'll learn. It's an identity you'll live.

By the end of this book, you won't just think differently. You'll move differently. Speak differently. Lead differently.

You'll become someone who:

- Doesn't wait for clarity—you take action and create it
- Doesn't freeze in fear—you flip it and use it as fuel
- Doesn't need confidence to begin—you build it by beginning
- Doesn't stand at the edge of the unknown—you cross the line
- Doesn't wait for perfect—you move forward anyway

People will describe you with awe in their voice: "They don't hesitate. They just FIO."

You'll join a movement of people who face challenges and say: "I don't know how yet—but I'll figure it out."

This isn't just a book. It's permission to stop waiting for permission.

You'll text your friends: "I FIO'd it!" after doing the scary thing. They might not know what it means at first—but they'll feel your energy.

You'll see someone stuck and say: "Just FIO...let me show you how!) Because you'll know their biggest enemy isn't failure—it's regret.

You'll join the doers. The starters. The movers. The ones with messy notes and legendary stories.

We start before we're ready. We figure it out through action. And we high-five each other at the finish line.

## This Is For You If...

You've been saying "maybe next year" about the same dream... for years.

You've got seventeen tabs open about how to start—but haven't started.

You know exactly what you want to do, you just keep waiting for it to feel less scary.

You're tired of your own excuses but don't know how to stop making them.

You've read every book about change but haven't changed.

You don't want your eulogy to say, "They had such potential."

This is for the overthinker who needs to become an over-doer. For the perfectionist who needs to fall in love with "good enough to start." For the spreadsheet lover who needs to close Excel and open the door.

This is for the person who's been living in the gap between who they are and who they want to be.

For anyone who doesn't want to sit in their rocking chair at 90 wondering "what if?"

This is for the person who has that ONE thing on their mind right now. You know the thing. The thing that made you pick up this book in the first place.

You're hoping this book will finally be the catalyst. You're hoping someone will give you permission. You're hoping to feel ready.

I'm here to tell you: The permission needs to come from you. The ready feeling doesn't exist. And the catalyst isn't this book—it's your decision to stop waiting.

That thing doesn't need more research, it needs you to FIO.

## What You'll Discover:

In this book, you'll discover:

- Why your brain keeps you stuck (and how to override it)
- The three-step FIO Loop that turns fear into fuel
- Real stories of how I FIO'd some of my craziest adventures
- How to build evidence that you can handle anything
- Why messy action beats perfect plans every time

You'll hear stories like:

- The night I created Rick's Run at 11:58 PM while ugly-crying through American Sniper
- Flying to Costa Rica with no plan and rescuing my daughter in under 15 hours
- Sending a pitch video to Jesse Itzler in under 3 hours—with no plan just pure belief and energy
- How people just like you decided they'd rather fail than keep wondering "what if."

By the time you finish this book, you won't just understand the FIO Mindset—you'll be living it.

## Your Fear Line Is Waiting

Your Fear Line is waiting. And it's been waiting long enough.

Put this book down for ten seconds. Text someone about that thing you've been avoiding. Just write: "I need to tell you something." Send it. Now pick this back up.

Feel that terror? Good.

Let's FIO.

# Part 1

# The Awakening

# 1

# THE SIMPLE TRUTH ABOUT WHY YOU'RE STUCK

"Whether you think you can, or you think you can't—you're right."

—Henry Ford

## Before We Dive In: Your 60-Second Crash Course on Mindset

I'm a mindset nerd. For twenty-five years, I've devoured everything—books, podcasts, YouTube videos, research papers. Personal growth and development, behavioral psychology, evolutionary psychology, neuroscience, goal-setting theory, peak performance. All the things, all the time.

Jim Rohn said it best: "Stand guard at the door of your mind." I took that literally. I've been the bouncer at my brain's door, only letting in content that teaches me how humans behave and change.

True confession: Understanding transformation has become my daily obsession. I don't just consume this stuff—I live it, test it, break it, rebuild it. I experiment on myself first, then apply what actually works to parenting, business, relationships, racing.

But here's the thing: You don't need twenty-five years of research to FIO. You don't need to understand evolutionary psychology or neuroplasticity or why your amygdala hijacks your prefrontal cortex when you're scared.

All those thousands of hours studying human behavior taught me one thing worth knowing:

There's a simple chain reaction running your life, and once you see it, you can change it:

**What you THINK repeatedly becomes what you BELIEVE. What you BELIEVE becomes your MINDSET. What your MINDSET is determines your ACTIONS. Your ACTIONS become your LIFE.**

That's it. That's the operating system. Read it again.

Most people try to change their actions without changing their thoughts. That's like trying to make your car go forward while it's in reverse. Lots of noise, no progress.

This chapter shows you how to shift gears.

Ready? Let's expose what's really keeping you stuck.

## The Invisible Glasses That Control Your Life

Every morning, you wake up and put on a pair of invisible glasses.

You don't realize you're doing it. You don't feel them on your face. But they're there, coloring everything you see, shaping every decision you make, determining whether you'll cross that fear line or stand at it forever.

These glasses? They're your mindset. And most people don't realize they're wearing the wrong prescription.

But here's what nobody tells you: Those glasses were prescribed by your thoughts. Thousands of them. Repeated daily. For years.

## The Formula That Runs Your Life

### Thoughts → Beliefs → Mindset → Action (or No Action)

That's the whole game.

Your repeated thoughts become your beliefs. Your beliefs create your mindset. Your mindset drives your actions. Your actions determine your life.

Let me show you exactly how this works:

### The Thought Loop That Keeps You Stuck:

- You think (1000x): "I always fail at things like this"
- This becomes the belief: "I'm someone who fails"
- Which creates the mindset: "Why even try?"
- Results in: No action. Couch. "someday-itis".

### The Thought Loop That Keeps You Preparing:

- You think (1000x): "I need to know more first"
- This becomes the belief: "I'm not ready yet"
- Which creates the mindset: "Just a little more preparation"
- Results in: Eternal research. Classic "someday-itis".

### The Thought Loop That Gets You Moving:

- You think (1000x): "I'll figure it out"
- This becomes the belief: "I'm resourceful"
- Which creates the mindset: "Start now, adjust later"
- Results in: Immediate action. FIO.

## Your Brain Is Building What You Think

Here's what neuroscience proves: Every thought you repeat physically changes your brain. Neural pathways that fire together, wire together. You're literally building highways for your most common thoughts.

Think "I'm not ready" fifty times a day? You've paved a superhighway for hesitation.

Think "I'll figure it out" fifty times a day? You've built an autobahn for action.

Your brain doesn't judge. It just builds what you repeat.

**The Three Paths Everyone Takes:**

**Path 1:**

### Limiting Thoughts → Limiting Beliefs → Fixed Mindset → No Action

Your thoughts: "I can't," "I'm not that type," "That's for other people"

Your belief: "I'm not a runner"

Your mindset: "Why even try?"

Your action: Stay on the couch.

This is the path of "I can't." These people have thought themselves into stone. Every "I can't" thought reinforced their limitations, until those limitations became their identity.

**Path 2:**

### Empowering Thoughts → Empowering Beliefs → Growth Mindset → Preparation

Your thoughts: "I could learn," "I need more information," "Almost ready"

Your belief: "I could run if I prepare"

Your mindset: "I need to be ready first"

Your action: Research, buy gear, plan, but never start

This is the path of "I'm not ready yet." Classic "someday-itis"— that chronic condition where everything important gets scheduled for a day that doesn't exist. These people know growth is possible but think it happens through preparation, not action.

## Path 3:

## Launching Thoughts → Launching Beliefs → FIO Mindset → Immediate Action

Your thoughts: "Let me try," "I'll adjust," "I'll figure it out"

Your belief: "I learn by doing"

Your mindset: "Start now"

Your action: Put on shoes and go

This is the path of "I'll figure it out." These people's thoughts have trained them that action creates clarity, not the other way around.

Here's what nobody tells you about your resistance to action: You're not lazy. You're not unmotivated. You're not broken.

Your brain is doing exactly what it evolved to do—keep you alive.

Your ancestors survived because they avoided unknown rustling bushes (might be a tiger), stayed with their tribe (safety in numbers), and didn't try new berries (might be poison).

**The ones who said "Let me go check out that saber-toothed tiger"? They didn't survive long enough to become your ancestors.**

Your brain's number one job isn't growth. It's survival. And survival loves one thing: the known. Even if the known is mediocre. Even if the known is killing your dreams. Your brain will choose familiar misery over unfamiliar possibility. Every. Single. Time.

## Your Brain's Protection Racket

When you're about to send that bold email, sign up for that race, have that conversation, or make that change, your amygdala (fear center) fires in 200 milliseconds. Before you consciously think "maybe I should," your brain has already sent ten "DANGER" signals through your body.

- Chest tightens (preparing for attack)
- Palms sweat (better grip for fighting or climbing)
- Stomach drops (blood diverts to major muscles)
- Thoughts race: "Not now," "Too risky," "Wait until..."

These aren't character flaws. They're features. Your brain is trying to save you from modern-day "tigers":

- Rejection (social death to your ancient brain)
- Failure (loss of status in the tribe)
- Embarrassment (expelled from the group)
- The unknown (definitely tigers)

## The Mismatch That Keeps You Stuck

Your brain can't tell the difference between a real tiger and posting a vulnerable video, asking for a raise, starting a business, or signing up for the Boston Marathon with no real running experience.

To your amygdala, they all scream "POSSIBLE DEATH."

But here's what your brain doesn't understand: Those aren't tigers anymore. In our world, the real danger isn't trying something new—it's staying exactly where you are. The predator isn't in the unknown. It's in your comfort zone, slowly devouring your potential one safe day at a time.

## You Can Override Your Wiring

The beautiful truth neuroscience proves: Your brain has neuroplasticity. It can rewire at any age.

Every time you take action despite the "danger" signals, you teach your brain: "That wasn't a tiger. We survived. We can do that again."

Every FIO loop literally rewires your threat detection system:

- First time sending a bold email: Full panic
- Tenth time: Mild discomfort
- Hundredth time: Tuesday

I know this is true because I've watched my own brain rewire over years of crossing fear lines.

The same brain that used to panic about making phone calls now picks up the phone without thinking twice.

The same brain that used to rehearse conversations for days now just has them.

The same brain that used to need permission from everyone before making a decision now trusts itself to choose.

Same brain. Different wiring.

And if I can rewire mine—starting from a place of significant fear and doubt—you can rewire yours.

The FIO Loop is the tool that makes that rewiring happen.

"Every time you complete the loop, you're not just taking action in the moment:"

## You're reprogramming your default response to fear.

Your brain isn't your enemy. It's your overprotective parent who still thinks you're five and everything is sharp or hot or definitely going to hurt you.

You don't need to fight it. You need to thank it and then override it: "Thanks for the warning, brain. I know

"Every time you complete the loop, you're not just taking action in the moment:"

That's what the FIO Loop does. It gives you a system to move through ancient fear with modern courage.

## Where Your Limiting Thoughts Came From

### The Stories You Never Chose to Believe

Before we dive into where your specific limiting thoughts came from, I need you to understand something crucial: Most of the beliefs running your life were installed before you were old enough to question them.

Think about it. By age seven, your brain had already absorbed thousands of messages about who you are, what you're capable of, and what's possible for "people like you." These messages came from everywhere—parents, teachers, TV, overheard conversations, playground interactions, even the look on someone's face when you tried something new.

Your young brain, desperate to keep you safe and help you belong, filed every rejection as danger, every criticism as truth, every limitation as law. It was doing its job—protecting you. But the protection that serves a seven-year-old becomes the prison that traps the adult.

Here's the thing: Your brain doesn't fact-check these beliefs. It just runs them on repeat, like outdated software you never asked to install.

Time to uninstall it.

"Change the way you look at things and the things you look at change." —Wayne Dyer

## The Origin Stories of Your Limitations

### That thought "I'm not creative?"

Maybe you were in third grade, bursting with an idea for the class play. You raised your hand so high you nearly fell out of your chair. When you shared your idea—something wild, something different—the teacher said, "Let's stick to something more... realistic." The class moved on. Your idea disappeared. And your brain filed away: *My ideas aren't good enough. Creative people have ideas that get picked. I'm not creative.*

Or maybe you watched the "creative kids" get praised for their stories, their inventions, their wild imagination, while you got praised for following directions, staying in the lines, being "good." Without anyone saying it directly, you learned: *There are creative people and there are rule-followers. I'm a rule-follower.*

Now, decades later, you still say "I'm not creative" like it's a fact, when really it's just a conclusion a nine-year-old made based on incomplete evidence.

### That thought "I'm bad with money?"

Maybe you grew up hearing hushed arguments through thin walls. Your parents' voices tight with stress, sharp with fear. "How are we going to pay for..." "We can't afford..." "Money doesn't grow on trees." Your nervous system learned: *Money = danger. Money = fights. Money = never enough.*

Or maybe you watched your parent's shoulders tense every time they opened a bill. Saw them avoid the mail. Noticed how the mood in the house shifted at the end of the month. Without anyone saying a word, you absorbed the message: *Money is scary. Better not look too close.*

Now you're an adult who avoids checking bank balances, who says "I'm bad with money" as if it's a permanent condition rather than a learned avoidance pattern from a kid trying to stay safe in a stressed household.

**That thought "I'm too much?"**

Maybe you were the kid who laughed too loud, felt too deeply, dreamed too big. Until someone—a parent, a teacher, a peer— said those two words that shrink souls: "Tone it down." "You're exhausting." "Do you always have to be so... extra?"

Your brightness made someone else uncomfortable, so they asked you to dim yourself. And because you wanted to belong more than you wanted to shine, you did. You learned to moderate your enthusiasm. Contain your energy. Apologize for your intensity. "Sorry, I know I'm a lot."

But you weren't too much. You were just more than they could handle. There's a difference.

**That thought "I have to be perfect before I start?"**

This one probably came wrapped in gold stars and good intentions. You learned early that A's meant approval. That mistakes meant red marks. That "good job" came after perfect performance, not brave attempts.

Nobody meant to teach you that your worth was contingent on your output. But every "I'm so proud of you" attached to an achievement taught you: *I'm loveable when I succeed.* Every "you can do better" taught you: *I'm not enough as I am.*

So now you won't start the business until the plan is flawless. Won't apply for the job unless you meet 100% of the qualifications. Won't share your work until it's perfect—which means never.

**That thought "People like me don't do things like that?"**

This might be the most insidious one, because it often came disguised as protection. "Let's be realistic." "Don't get your hopes up." "Stay in your lane." "Know your place."

Maybe it was socioeconomic: "We're not college people." Maybe it was gendered: "That's not what girls/boys do." Maybe it was cultural: "That's not how our family does things." Maybe it was geographic: "People from here don't end up there."

These boundaries were drawn around you before you knew you could cross them. They became invisible fences you still honor, decades later.

## The Truth About These Hand-Me-Down Beliefs

Here's what nobody told you: These beliefs aren't yours. They're hand-me-downs, like old clothes that never fit right. You've been wearing someone else's fears, someone else's limitations, someone else's small dreams.

Your parents' money fears? Those belonged to their experience, not yours. Your teacher's limited view of creativity? That was about her definition, not your potential. The person who said you were too much? They were really saying they weren't enough.

Most of our beliefs weren't chosen. They were absorbed. Inherited. Picked up from childhood, culture, comparison, criticism, or chaos. We collected them like stones in our pockets, and now we wonder why it's so hard to run.

## The Power to Choose Again

But here's the revolutionary truth: Just because a belief was handed to you doesn't mean you have to keep holding it.

You are not required to keep believing what a scared seven-year-old decided was true. You don't have to honor the limitations someone else put on you. You can put down beliefs that were never yours to carry.

Right now, today, this very second, you can choose new thoughts.

Not "someday when I've done more therapy." Not "once I've healed my inner child." Not "after I understand where it all came from." Now.

Because thoughts are not facts. Beliefs are not laws. They're just sentences you've been repeating so long you forgot they were optional.

You get to decide what runs your life now. The seven-year-old who decided you weren't creative doesn't get to make your decisions anymore. The teenager who learned to play small doesn't get to choose your dreams. The young adult who absorbed "not enough" doesn't get to set your limits.

You're the adult now. You get to choose.

And if you choose to believe you can FIO anything?

Well, then you can.

## The Missing Piece I Found in Applying Growth Mindset

Carol Dweck's revolutionary research on growth mindset fundamentally changed how we understand human potential. Her work proved what many suspected but couldn't articulate: our abilities aren't fixed. Intelligence isn't static. Talent isn't destiny. We can grow, adapt, evolve. (If you haven't read *Mindset: The*

*New Psychology of Success*, put it on your list. Dweck's research is the foundation that makes everything else possible—including what I'm about to share with you.)

But after twenty-two years of directing races and watching thousands of people at literal and metaphorical starting lines, I noticed something Dweck's framework doesn't fully address: the gap between believing you can grow and actually growing.

I saw it everywhere. Brilliant people who understood growth mindset, who could quote the research, who genuinely believed in their capacity to change—standing perfectly still. They had the mindset. They had the knowledge. What they didn't have was momentum.

That's when I realized: Growth mindset is necessary but not sufficient for some. It opens the door, but something else has to walk you through it.

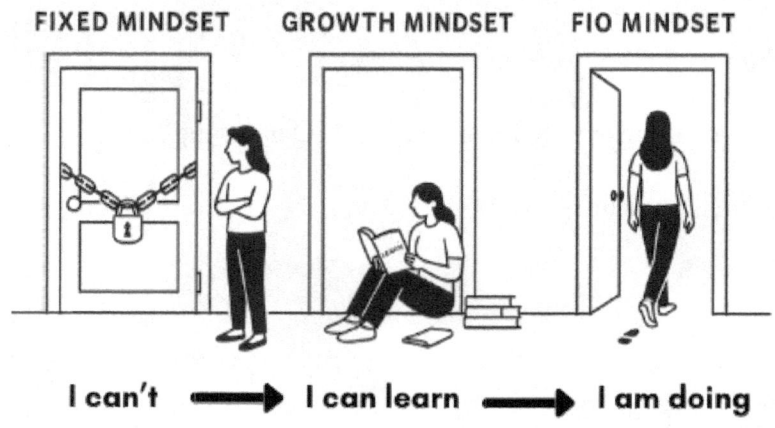

FIXED MINDSET   GROWTH MINDSET   FIO MINDSET

I can't ➡ I can learn ➡ I am doing

## The Critical Distinction between the Growth and FIO Mindsets

Here's the difference that changes everything:

**Growth Mindset proves the mountain is climbable**

**FIO Mindset gets you to climb.**

Think about it: Here are just a few more examples of how the two mindsets differ:

- Growth Mindset: "I can learn to run marathons" → *researches training plans*
- FIO Mindset: "I'll learn by running" → *signs up for next week's 5K*
- Growth Mindset: "I can develop as a writer" → *reads books about writing*
- FIO Mindset: "I'll develop by writing" → *publishes imperfect blog post today*
- Growth Mindset: "I'm capable of learning business" → *enrolls in another course*
- FIO Mindset: "I'll learn by doing business" → *makes first sale, however messy*

One is about potential. The other is about evidence.

One collects information. The other collects experience.

One believes in possibility. The other creates proof.

Growth mindset is the permission slip. FIO is showing up to class.

## The Confidence Paradox Nobody Discusses

Here's what the self-help industry won't tell you: Confidence isn't a prerequisite—it's a byproduct.

When I pitched Jesse Itzler, I wasn't confident. When I ran the Boston Marathon with lingering bronchitis, I wasn't confident. When I started Rick's Run at midnight, I wasn't confident.

My confidence came after taking the first steps. The doing generated the confidence, I didn't wait for the confidence before starting.

Every time you FIO, you create a breadcrumb trail of proof. Your brain starts to recognize a pattern: *I've figured things out before. I can figure this out too.*

That's not motivational speaking. That's neuroplasticity in action. Your brain literally rewires based on evidence, not affirmations.

The formula isn't: Get confident → Take action → Succeed

It's: Take action → Collect evidence → Update identity → Become confident

## The 24-Hour Mirror

Put this book down. Close your eyes. Think about yesterday— every decision you made, every action you postponed, every opportunity you considered.

What thoughts drove those choices?

Did your mind whisper variations of "not yet"—I'm not ready, I need to learn more, the timing isn't right, I don't have enough resources?

Or did it push you forward with "let's try"—I'll figure it out, good enough to start, I'll learn by doing?

Here's what most people never realize: Your most practiced thoughts become your most predictable outcomes. The sentences that ran through your head yesterday are writing your tomorrow. They're not just thoughts. They're architects, building your future one repeated belief at a time.

## The Three Paths Revealed in Thought

Your dominant thought pattern has already chosen your path—probably years ago, without asking your permission.

**Path 1** lives in the language of impossibility: "I can't." "I'm not the kind of person who..." "That's impossible for someone like me." These thoughts create permanent paralysis. The car isn't just parked—the engine's been removed.

**Path 2** speaks fluent preparation: "I need to learn more first." "I am almost ready." "After I master this next skill." These thoughts feel productive, even noble. But they're a sophisticated form of standing still—motion without movement, like running on a treadmill in a room with an open door.

**Path 3** operates in a different dialect entirely: "Let me try." "I'll figure it out." "What's the smallest step I can take right now?" These thoughts don't wait for certainty. They create it through action.

The devastating truth nobody wants to admit? All three paths demand the same energy. Staying stuck is just as exhausting as moving forward—the anxiety, the mental gymnastics, the energy spent defending your inaction. The only difference is what you have to show for that exhaustion.

## The Revolution in Your Head

Your brain is going to resist what comes next because it threatens everything it's built to keep you safe.

You can switch paths right now.

Not next Monday. Not after you finish this book. Not when you feel ready. Right now, in this moment, before you turn this page.

This isn't wishful thinking. It's neuroscience. Your brain is constantly rewiring based on what you feed it. Every thought you repeat carves a deeper groove. Every new thought creates a new possibility.

You don't need a year of therapy to change a thought (though therapy does have tremendous value). You don't need perfect understanding (though learning always helps). You don't need to feel ready—that feeling is a myth successful people made up after they'd already succeeded.

You need **one** new thought, repeated until your brain accepts it as truth.

## The Addition Method That Changes Everything

Here's the secret to thought revolution: Don't fight your limiting beliefs. That's exhausting and usually backfires. Instead, become a mental editor. Add a second clause to every limiting thought:

The thought "I'm not ready" becomes "I'm not ready, but I'll start small."

The thought "I don't know how" becomes "I don't know how, but I can figure out the first step."

The thought "What if I fail?" becomes "What if I fail? But what if this works?"

The thought "I'm not qualified" becomes "I'm not qualified, but neither was anyone on day one."

You're not denying reality. You're expanding it. You're showing your brain that the story it's been telling is incomplete. There's a "but" it hasn't considered. A possibility it hasn't explored.

Your brain can handle this kind of gentle revolution. It's like adding a window to a room that's always been dark—suddenly, there's another view.

---

## CHAPTER 1 TAKEAWAY

You're living on one of three paths. Your thoughts put you there. Only Path 3 moves forward. The difference between stuck and unstoppable isn't talent, timing, or luck—it's the thoughts you've practiced most.

## YOUR CHAPTER 1 ACTION

Identify your most limiting thought—the one that shows up uninvited every time you consider changing. Write it down. Now write what you'll think instead, starting with the same words but adding, " but..."

Put that new thought where you'll see it tomorrow morning. Your bathroom mirror. Your coffee maker. Your phone's lock screen.

That's it. Simple, unglamorous; yet revolutionary.

The FIO Loop I'm about to teach you is the system for staying on Path 3. But first, I need to show you something that might disturb you—the real price you're paying for waiting. Not the motivational speaker version. The mathematical truth.

Turn the page. Let's calculate what someday is actually costing you.

Waiting is fear wearing a three-piece suit, pretending to be wisdom.

# 2

# THE COST OF WAITING

"The Cost of Waiting is Paid in Regret"
— Rachel Martin

# You Know Your Path. Now What?

Last chapter, you identified which path you're on.

You saw how Path 1 (I can't) keeps you stuck forever. How Path 2 (I'm not ready yet) keeps you preparing forever. How Path 3 (I'll figure it out) gets you moving.

But understanding isn't doing.

Most people close books like this thinking "Great ideas!" then go right back to waiting. Why? Because they don't realize what staying on Path 1 or Path 2 actually costs them.

They think waiting is neutral—like hitting pause on Netflix. You can just come back later, right?

Wrong. So wrong it hurts.

## The Two Lives You Are Living

Right now, you're not living one life. You're living two. And the gap between them is exhausting you.

### Life #1: Your Actual Life

This is where you wake up every morning. Where you're reading this book. Where you keep saying "someday" and "not yet" and "when I'm ready."

In your actual life, you're still thinking about:

- That business you want to start
- That conversation you need to have
- That race you keep bookmarking
- That dream gathering dust

You're still at the starting line. Still preparing. Still waiting.

**Life #2: The Life You Wish You Were Living**

This is the life you see when you can't sleep at 3 AM. The one where you already started. Already had the conversation. Already crossed the finish line.

In the life you wish you were living:

- That business? It's two years old with actual clients
- That conversation? It happened and you have clarity
- That race? There's a medal on your wall
- That dream? You're living it

The life you wish you were living isn't vague. You can see it perfectly. You've imagined it a thousand times. You know exactly what it looks like, feels like, even smells like.

## The Gap That's Growing Every Day

Here's what makes this so hard: You can see both lives clearly. But you're only living one.

Every day you don't act, the life you wish you were living moves forward without you. It keeps growing, evolving, succeeding— while you stand still in your actual life watching it pull away.

That gap between your actual life and the life you wish you were living?

### *That's regret forming in real-time.*

Not when you're 90 looking back. Right now. Today. In this moment.

## Why Living Split Is Exhausting

You can't fully commit to your actual life because you know it's not what you want.

You can't fully live the life you wish you were living because it only exists in your head.

So you live in the gap between them. Half in, half out. Split. Exhausted.

Going to bed in one life, dreaming of another, waking up disappointed. Every. Single. Day.

The life you wish you were living doesn't pause while you "get ready."

While you're reading one more book, that other life's business is two years ahead. While you're waiting for courage, that other you already has stories to tell. While you're preparing, the life you wish you were living is happening without you.

The longer you wait, the wider the gap. The wider the gap, the more it aches. The more it aches, the harder it feels to close.

## The Lies We Tell Ourselves

You already know what you want. But you keep waiting.

You tell yourself you'll do it when you have more time. But you won't have more time—you'll have different time.

You tell yourself you need to be more prepared. But you're just preparing to prepare to prepare.

You tell yourself you'll start once things settle down. But things don't settle—they just change flavors of chaos.

You tell yourself you're too busy. But you scrolled for three hours last night.

These excuses sound responsible. Your friends probably nod supportively when you say them.

But after twenty-two years of jumping before I felt ready, here's what I know: Waiting is rarely about preparation. It's fear wearing a three-piece suit, pretending to be wisdom.

## The Hidden Invoice of Hesitation

Most people think inaction is neutral. "If I don't do it now, I'll do it later."

But inaction isn't neutral. It's expensive. And you're paying for it in a currency you can't earn back: Time.

## Every time you hesitate, you:

**Miss opportunities with expiration dates.** That perfect moment has a shelf life. Markets shift. People move on. Doors close.

**Train yourself to be someone who doesn't.** Your brain builds highways for behaviors you repeat. Choose "later" enough times and your brain's GPS will always route you directly to Procrastination Station.

**Give fear a promotion.** Each time you back down, fear gets more powerful. Pretty soon it's CEO of your life decisions. Dr. Sean Young, UCLA professor and author of *Stick with It*, explains: "Your brain becomes more efficient at what you practice. If you practice procrastination, you become a professional procrastinator."

You're literally strengthening Path 1 or Path 2 every time you wait.

So, stop waiting. Start strengthening the right one.

The cost of waiting is invisible…until it shows up as the life you never lived.

# The Night Everything Changed: Rick's Run

March 23, 2016. 11:58 PM.

I'd just finished watching American Sniper, alone on my couch, wrapped in my dad's hideously ugly 1970's afghan—browns and oranges with pills that begged to be picked off.

I was sobbing. Not pretty tears. The shoulder-shaking, nose-clogging, can't-breathe kind.

Chris Kyle's story cracked something open in me. His struggle with the weight of war—it was my dad's story.

My dad was a Vietnam vet who carried invisible wounds. He'd look for snipers on trips to buy milk. Couldn't sleep in beds, only chairs with the TV on. The war never really ended for him.

After he died, I'd been talking about creating a race in his honor. For years.

Talking. Planning. Living with "someday-itis".

But that night, wrapped in his ugly blanket, one question hit me:

**"What the heck am I waiting for?"**

My dad didn't get to wait. Veterans struggling right now don't have the luxury of "someday."

So right there, at 11:58 PM on a Tuesday, still in my pajamas with mascara everywhere, I pulled out my laptop.

Emailed the timing company. Emailed the announcer. I opened my calendar and picked Memorial Day.

I jumped from Path 2 to Path 3 in one moment. From "I'll do it when I'm ready" to "I'm figuring it out right now."

Rick's Run was born.

Today? Rick's Run has raised tens of thousands of dollars for veterans support. Kids wear their medals to school on the Tuesday after, beaming with pride. The local veterans know someone gives a damn.

None of it—not a single dollar, not a single smile, not a single thank you—would exist if I'd stayed on Path 2 that night.

## What Science Says About Regret

Dr. Thomas Gilovich, psychology professor at Cornell University and author of research published in *Psychological Review*, interviewed hundreds of people in their 70s, 80s, and 90s about their biggest regrets.

**76% said their biggest regrets were things they DIDN'T do.**

Not their failures. Not their mistakes. Rather the chances they didn't take.

Gilovich explains: "When we fail at something we tried, we can process it. Learn from it. Find meaning in the attempt. But when we never try? There's no closure. Just an endless 'what if' that haunts us."

Regrets of inaction:

- Last longer than regrets of action
- Intensify over time (while action regrets fade)
- Create more "what if" rumination
- Generate deeper emotional pain

Why? Because when you try and fail, you know what happened. When you never try, your imagination tortures you with infinite possibilities.

## The Compound Cost Nobody Calculates

The cost of waiting isn't just the opportunity you miss. It's everything that would have come after.

When I finally started Rick's Run, I didn't just create one race. That one action created:

- Relationships with sponsors who supported other projects
- Skills I used dozens of times since
- Credibility that opened new doors
- Confidence for every subsequent fear line
- A community that became part of everything else

If I'd waited, I wouldn't have just delayed a race. I'd have delayed becoming who I am now.

Think of waiting like compound interest in reverse. When you invest early, money grows exponentially. Opportunities work the same way.

But when you wait? You're not just missing the opportunity. You're missing the person you would become by taking it.

## But I'm Already Behind

I hear this constantly. "I'm 45 and haven't started." "Everyone my age has it figured out." "It's too late for me."

Let's pause for a moment: What do chicken, fashion, and literature all have to do with one another?

Have you heard of Colonel Sanders? He was 62—living in his car, visiting restaurants, cooking his chicken recipe for anyone who'd taste it—when he started franchising KFC.

Vera Wang? She was 40 when she launched her bridal empire—after spending two decades working for other people's fashion brands.

Laura Ingalls Wilder? She was 65 when she published her first Little House book—after a lifetime of farming, struggle, and stories she'd been carrying for decades.

But forget famous people. Let me tell you about me:

- 30 when I ran my first road race which was a full marathon
- 38 when I became a race director with no experience.
- 44 when I pitched Jesse Itzler (terrified)
- 48 when I wrote this book (first time author)

The only "too late" is when you're dead. Everything else is just "not yet."

Every day you wait because you think it's "too late" is another day you kick the can of your dreams further down the road.

If you're reading this at 25: Start now before fear calcifies into habit.

If you're reading this at 40: Start now with all the wisdom you've gathered.

If you're reading this at 60: Start now because you know how fast time moves.

If you're reading this at 75: Start now because you're proof it's never too late.

The perfect time doesn't exist. The right age doesn't exist. "Too late" doesn't exist. Only today exists.

## Real People Who Stopped Waiting:

I surveyed my community—athletes, entrepreneurs, dreamers who finally made their move. I asked about their bold leaps, their regrets, their lessons.

The results:

**92% said their biggest regret was not starting sooner,** not that they started. That regretted WAITING to start.

**87% said they weren't "ready" when they began.** They figured it out as they went. Every single one.

**73% said fear almost stopped them completely.** The fear never went away. They just moved anyway.

**100% said they're glad they finally did it, not** 99%. One hundred percent. No exceptions.

**0% said "I wish I'd waited longer"** Zero. Nobody. Not one person.

### How to Close the Gap

The canyon between your two lives feels impossible to cross. Standing at the edge, you can see the other side—the life where you've already started the business, had the conversation, made the change. But from here, it might as well be on another planet.

Here's what I learned after twenty-two years of watching people at this exact precipice: You don't need to jump the entire canyon.

You don't need wings. You don't need to wait until the canyon shrinks.

You need to take one step that moves your actual life an inch closer to the life you wish you were living.

The FIO Loop becomes your bridge—not something you leap across, but something you return to, again and again, as you close the distance between intention and reality.

Every day you don't move, the imaginary version of your life keeps expanding while your real life quietly contracts. The gap grows. Not because you failed—but because waiting is still a choice.

So you move.

Not perfectly.

Not dramatically.

But deliberately.

You take a step. You pay attention to what happens. You adjust. You let the win register before rushing past it. That part matters more than most people realize—your brain needs evidence that progress is real.

Then you return.

Another hesitation loosened. Another decision made from trust instead of fear. Another inch reclaimed.

Day by day, return by return, something shifts. Your actual life starts catching up. The phantom life you've been maintaining in your head begins to merge with reality. What once felt like a permanent divide starts to close.

Until one quiet morning—no announcement, no fireworks—you realize you're not living two lives anymore. You integrated. You became whole.

The life you're living is the life you once only imagined.

## Your Two Options

Let me be uncomfortably direct about what happens next.

**Option 1:** Stay on Path 1 or 2. Keep your excuses polished and ready. Tell yourself next year will be different while doing nothing different. Watch the gap between your actual life and your desired life become a canyon so wide you can no longer see across it.

In five years, you'll be explaining to someone younger why you never started. You'll use the same reasons you're using today. They'll nod politely while thinking what you're thinking right now about someone else: "That could have been different."

**Option 2:** Jump to Path 3. Not gracefully. Not when you're ready. Not with a perfect plan. Jump messy, uncertain, unprepared. Decide that waiting ends with this paragraph.

In five years, you'll be telling the story of how you started before you were ready. How the first steps were disasters. How you figured it out as you went. And someone will look at you the way you look at people living their actual dreams—with a mixture of admiration and "I wish I could do that."

The difference between these two futures isn't talent, luck, or circumstances. It's which option you choose in the next sixty seconds.

## The Compound Cost

The cost of waiting isn't just the opportunity you miss today. It compounds:

Each day you wait, you lose not just that day's progress but all the progress that would have built on it. The confidence you would have gained. The connections you would have made. The skills you would have developed. The stories you would have collected.

But there's a deeper cost, one that keeps me up at night when I think about all the people living at 40% of their potential:

You lose the person you were supposed to become.

Every day of waiting changes you—not into someone better, but into someone who's comfortable with a gap between who you are and who you could be. You become an expert at explaining why you haven't instead of someone who figures out how you can.

---

YOUR CHAPTER 2 TAKEAWAY

The gap between your two lives grows or shrinks based on what you do today. Not tomorrow. Not Monday. Today. Waiting isn't neutral—it's widening the canyon.

YOUR CHAPTER 2 ACTION

Right now—not after you finish this chapter, right now—answer this:

What's one thing you've been waiting to do?

_____

How long have you been waiting? _____

If you wait another year, who will you become?

_____

What's ONE action you could take before you go to bed tonight?

_____


Set a phone alarm for 8 PM titled "Did I take my inch?"

If you can't name one action, you're choosing the gap. If you can name it but won't do it, you're choosing the gap. The gap only closes through action, and action only happens now.

_____

The clock isn't just ticking—it's stealing. Every hour you spend preparing to live is an hour you're not living.

Turn the page. Let me show you exactly how the three paths play out in real life, and why only one leads to the person you're capable of becoming.

That gap between your actual life and the life you wish you were living? That's regret forming in real-time.

# Part II
# Activate

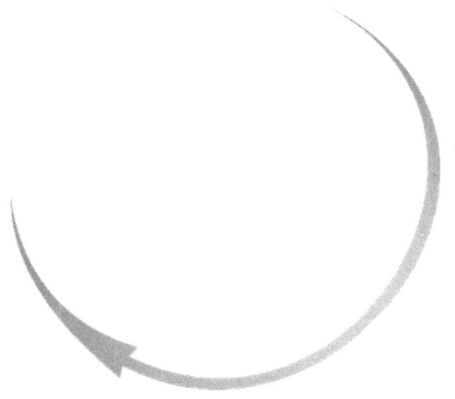

# 3

# THE FIO LOOP

## Your Three-Step System for Unstoppable Action

"The best time to plant a tree was 20 years ago. The second-best time is now."
— Chinese Proverb

You just saw what waiting costs you. The compound effect. The regret math. The neural pathways growing stronger every day you don't act.

You know which path you're on. You understand why your brain keeps you there.

Now let me show you the system that breaks the waiting pattern forever.

It's the same system that moves you from Path 1 or Path 2 straight to Path 3—and keeps you there.

It's what happens when Launching Beliefs turn into actual movement.

It took me from Instagram DM to Jesse Itzler partnership in 2 hours and 53 minutes. Let me show you exactly how I FIO'd it.

**December 6, 2021, 6:37 AM.**

I sent Jesse Itzler a DM on Instagram.

Not an email. Not a carefully crafted proposal. A DM.

By 9:34 AM—2 hours and 53 minutes later—I'd sent him a four-minute iPhone video about who I was, what I did, and how I could help promote All Day Running Co. to my athletes. No script. No makeup. Just me, propping my phone on top of my TV cabinet, being aggressively cheerful about my events, my community, and the philanthropy behind it all.

His response: "Amazing. I'll circle back post holiday!!!!!! Love what you are doing and congrats on all".

That response gave me the courage to pitch something bigger. On December 28th, I sent him my Hell on the Hill Maine Edition idea—before we'd even met face-to-face. I had been figuring everything out on my own for my events company already- from the design work to the finish lines…googled how to do it all, so I had the capabilities to send a pitch with logos, graphics, examples of swag…all of it.

Then came the Zoom call. Which is how I found myself sitting in front of my computer wearing a white ski helmet, clicking the Google Meet link.

Why the helmet? Glad you asked. In all my googling, I'd seen Jesse's post about wearing a wig to an important meeting with wife, Sara Blakely (Side note: Sara is another mentor who doesn't know doesn't know she's my mentor. She took $5000 and an idea..... and created SPANX® Then became one of the first woman self-made billionaires. Sara later founded SNEEX™, a luxury hybrid heel company. She designed a 78mm stiletto with the engineering of a sneaker. I would eventually cheer for 8 hours straight in these heels at RUNNINGMAN™ 2025, but that's a later story.) Jesse's message: "Not everything has to be so serious. Laugh at yourself. Have fun. Fun is important. And most of the time fun is super memorable!"

**Message received: Be memorable.**

That first call led to a collaboration with his All Day Running Co. team to help produce Hell on the Hill Maine Edition. This local event led to me becoming the race director for the race portion of their signature event, RUNNINGMAN™ 2023. Since then, I continue to help with this transformational event. Using the FIO Mindset, I ended up cheering for 10 hours straight on a one-mile track that first year (story coming later!) because that's who I am now. I love being someone who cheers until their voice gives out, hands throbbing from giving 1000's of high fives and power-ups, and keeps going anyway. I actually need to

FIO how to keep track of all of the high fives given…if you FIO, please send ideas my way!

This all materialized because I took 2 hours and 53 minutes to FIO instead of spending months perfecting a pitch that might never have been sent.

**Here's what changed everything:**

I focused on the opportunity and the potential results instead of the fear of the process.

That's the FIO Loop in action.

Three steps. Rinse. Repeat. Watch your life change.

"In any given moment we have two options: To step forward into growth or step back into safety."

— Abraham Maslow

# THE FIO LOOP: YOUR PATH 3 SYSTEM

Remember Chapter 1?

Path 3 people move immediately because of their Launching Beliefs. They commit to figuring it out instead of relying on the the confidence they already know how.

The FIO Loop is HOW they do it. It's the system that turns that launching belief into actual movement.

Here's how it worked with Jesse:

## F: FACE THE FEAR & FLIP IT

My brain screamed: "Who are you to pitch Jesse Itzler? He's sold companies to Warren Buffett. You don't live in that world. You'll embarrass yourself."

Classic Path 1 thinking trying to pull me back.

I flipped it: "What if he's looking for exactly this? What if this brings value to his community? What if this is the beginning of something amazing?"

That's the flip—taking your brain's worst-case scenario and asking "what's the best-case scenario?"

Both are equally possible. Why not focus on the one that moves you forward?

## I: IDENTIFY ONE ACTION

My action? I Googled "how to pitch to Jesse Itzler."

That's it. Not "create a perfect pitch deck."Not "hire a PR firm." Just one small action that moved me from thinking to doing.

I found an interview where he said he decides within 30 seconds if someone has the right energy. I realized a normal email wouldn't cut it. I needed video.

Problem: I didn't know how to send a video via email. Solution: I started typing into Google "how to send a video via email." Answer: Vimeo.

Next Google: "how to upload a video to Vimeo."

Four-minute video. Two takes. Done.

**O: OBSERVE, OPTIMIZE & CELEBRATE**

His response came fast. He was interested.

Observe: The imperfect, authentic video worked. Speed beat perfection.

Optimize: Trust my gut even more. Move even faster next time.

Celebrate: I pitched Jesse Itzler in under 3 hours and he responded! I didn't die! I FIO'd it!

**Each celebration makes the next loop easier. Your brain starts to crave the action instead of avoiding it.**

Two hours and 53 minutes. That's all it took to change everything. What could you do in the next 3 hours?

## Why It's A Loop And Not A Straight Line

Most action frameworks are linear. Do step one, then two, then three, then you're done.

The FIO Loop is different. It's built for repetition.

You don't FIO once and you're done. You do it again. And again. And again.

One loop = tiny courage muscle Ten loops = noticeable momentum Hundred loops = you're a different person

Remember from Chapter 2 how your brain builds highways? Every day you wait, you're strengthening the hesitation highway. But every FIO Loop builds a new trail for action.

Eventually, action becomes the highway. Hesitation becomes the overgrown path that no longer serves you.

## The Three Steps in Depth:

### F: FACE THE FEAR & FLIP IT

Fear isn't a stop sign—it's a GPS coordinate showing you where growth lives.

Remember those fear lines from the introduction? Every fear is just pointing to your next level.

When fear shows up (and it always will), most people hear:

- "What if I fail?"
- "What if I look stupid?"
- "What if I'm not ready?"

These thoughts feel like protection. In truth though they're actually a prison. Classic Path 1 and Path 2 thinking.

The flip forces you to ask different questions:

- "What if I succeed?"
- "What if this inspires others?"
- "What if I'm exactly who should do this?"

This isn't toxic positivity. It's recognizing that your brain serves up worst-case scenarios like they're facts. The "flip" reminds you that best-case scenarios are just as possible—often more likely.

Remember from the previous chapter that your brain evolved to scan for threats. It thinks keeping you on Path 1 or 2 keeps you safe. The "flip" interrupts that ancient wiring. It forces your prefrontal cortex (your thinking brain) to engage instead of letting your amygdala run the show.

### I: IDENTIFY ONE ACTION (THE SMALLER THE BETTER)

You don't need to see step ten. You just need to see step one.

Right now. Not tomorrow. Not after coffee. Now.

Tony Robbins says: "Never leave the site of a goal without taking action toward it."

But here's where people mess up: They think the decision is the hard part. It's not. The hard part is deciding again every five minutes when self-doubt sneaks back in.

That's why small, immediate action matters—it interrupts hesitation before it hardens into a habit.

When I wanted to pitch Jesse: First action? Google "how to pitch to Jesse Itzler."

When I wanted to create Rick's Run: First action? Pick a date on the calendar.

When I wanted to write this book: First action? Write one paragraph.

The action doesn't need to be perfect. It doesn't need to guarantee success. It just needs to turn "thinking about it" into momentum.

**Clarity comes from motion, not meditation.**

You don't need confidence first. You need movement first. Confidence is what follows when you prove to yourself that you can handle whatever comes next.

This is why Path 3 works—action creates evidence, evidence creates confidence, confidence creates more action.

### O: OBSERVE, OPTIMIZE & CELEBRATE

This step is where the magic compounds.

**Observe without judgment:** Not "I failed" or "I succeeded." Just "Here's what happened." You're collecting data, not writing your obituary.

**Optimize based on data:** What worked? What didn't? What's next? This isn't about perfection—it's about progression.

**Celebrate that you moved:** This isn't optional. Your brain needs the dopamine hit to want to do it again.

Most people only celebrate outcomes. FIO'ers celebrate movement.

- Sent the scary email? Celebrate.
- Made the imperfect video? Celebrate.
- Took the messy action? CELEBRATE.

Remember that neurons that fire together, wire together. You're literally training your brain to crave action instead of avoid it.

This step prevents two common traps:

**Trap 1: Blaming external factors.** "The timing was bad." "They didn't understand." These explanations kill momentum because they put control outside of you.

**Trap 2: Taking failure as identity.** "See? I knew I wasn't ready." "This proves I'm not cut out for this." These interpretations stop you from trying again.

The FIO Loop asks different questions:

- "What can I learn from this?"
- "What worked that I can repeat?"
- "What didn't work that I can adjust?"
- "What's my next move?"

Every outcome—even the disappointing ones—becomes valuable data for your next loop.

## How The Loop Rewires Your Brain

Remember how your brain is constantly strengthening neural pathways? The FIO Loop hijacks that process to work in your favor.

When you consistently cycle through the loop, three powerful processes occur:

### 1. FEAR RESPONSE REWIRING

Each time you face a fear, flip it, and take action anyway, you're teaching your amygdala: "This thing we're afraid of? We've done it before. We survived. Maybe it's not as dangerous as we thought."

Over time, your amygdala becomes less reactive. The alarm still sounds, but at a lower volume. This is why the tenth time you do something scary is easier than the first.

## 2. ACTION-REWARD PATHWAYS

Each time you take action and celebrate it, your brain releases dopamine. This creates what neuroscientists call a "success spiral" by strengthening the neural pathways associated with action.

Your brain essentially says: "Hey, that action you took? It felt good. Let's make it easier to do that again."

## 3. NEURAL PATTERN FORMATION

Dr. Donald Hebb's principle that "neurons that fire together, wire together" helps illustrate why consistent use of the FIO Loop literally reshapes your brain to favor action over hesitation.

Right now, if you're on Path 1 or 2, hesitation is your highway. The loop doesn't erase that pathway—but it builds a new one. Every loop makes the action pathway stronger and the hesitation pathway weaker.

# Why the Complete Loop Matters

You might be thinking: "Can't I just focus on one part? Maybe just identifying actions?"

Here's why that doesn't work:

The loop tackles the complete cycle of meaningful action:

- **Fear (step 1)** - addresses the emotional barrier keeping you on Path 1 or 2
- **Decision paralysis (step 2)** - provides the bridge from Path 2's eternal preparation to Path 3's immediate action
- **Learning and momentum (step 3)** - ensures you stay on Path 3 instead of sliding back

Miss any step, and you create a weak link.

Skip the flip, and fear pulls you back to Path 1. Skip identifying immediate action, and you're stuck on Path 2 forever. Skip observing and celebrating, and you miss the brain rewiring that makes Path 3 your new default.

Each successful loop makes the next loop easier:

- Loop once: You prove you can jump to Path 3
- Loop five times: Path 3 starts feeling natural
- Loop twenty times: Action becomes your default response
- Loop a hundred times: You can't imagine living any other way

## Your Turn: Start Looping Today

Remember at the end of the previous chapter you identified what waiting was costing you. You saw your specific regret math.

Now it's time to break that pattern.

Don't wait until you finish the book. Don't wait until you understand every nuance. Start now.

Think of that thing from Chapter 2—the one you've been putting off. Run it through one complete cycle of The FIO Loop:

**1. FACE YOUR FEAR AND FLIP IT:** What are you actually afraid might happen? Write it down. Now flip that into a positive possibility.

**2. IDENTIFY ONE IMMEDIATE ACTION:** What's one small step you could take right now—before you finish this chapter? Not the perfect action. The smallest action that moves you from Path 2 to Path 3.

**3. OBSERVE, OPTIMIZE AND CELEBRATE:** After you take that action, observe what happened without judgment. What can you learn? What's your next move? Acknowledge that you completed the loop. You just jumped to Path 3!

This simple practice, repeated consistently, will make Path 3 your new normal.

Remember: you don't need to do it perfectly. You just need to do it.

The loop works when you work it.

So let's go.

### Chapter 3 Takeaways

- The FIO Loop is your system for living on Path 3—turning Launching Beliefs into immediate action
- The three steps work together: Face the Fear & Flip It, Identify One Action, Observe/Optimize/Celebrate
- Each loop physically rewires your brain, weakening Path 1 and 2 patterns while strengthening Path 3
- The loop works in any context—from pitching Jesse Itzler to everyday challenges
- It's designed for repetition: the power comes from cycling through continuously
- The loop is what keeps you on Path 3 instead of sliding back to old patterns
- Action—not perfection—creates results

**YOUR FIO ACTION STEP**

Before you move to the next chapter, complete one full cycle of the FIO Loop with something real in your life.

Use that thing from Chapter 2 that's been costing you. The one where you calculated your regret math.

Run it through all three steps, and take that first action before you continue reading.

The rest of this book will be far more valuable once you've experienced jumping from Path 2 to Path 3—even if that first loop feels messy or uncertain.

The loop works when you work it.

So let's go.

When you flip your fear from "What if I fail?" to "What if I succeed?", you're not just changing a thought.

*You're changing your entire operating system from one that protects to one that propels.*

# 4

## Face the Fear and Flip It

"Doubt kills more dreams than failure ever will." — Suzy Kassem

# The Storm that Changed Everything

The first time I crewed Race Across America, I had no idea what I was getting into. Let me remind you of what RAAM is: It's a 3,000-mile, nonstop ultra-endurance event where teams and solo riders race coast to coast—from California to Maryland—without stopping. No stages. No rest days. Just a relentless clock, an open road, and a battle against exhaustion, terrain, and time.

It was 2021. My very first RAAM. The first of 3 years in a row that I would crew for this insane event.

Somewhere deep in the Navajo Nation, just after midnight, an intense storm rolled in. I mean STORM. The kind that makes the hair on your arms stand up. Lightning cracked across the desert sky like a strobe light. Wind howling so loud I could barely hear myself think. Dust swirling. Adrenaline pumping. My hands were shaking as I stood outside the van, waiting for the next rider exchange.

I was new. I was scared. And it was dawning on me that this race—this wild, unrelenting race—never stops for anything. Not weather. Not nightfall. Not fear.

And I didn't know what to do.

Do we shelter our riders and wait this out? Do we call it in? Do we even have that option?

So I asked Ben. Ben was one of our riders—a seasoned ultra-endurance athlete. Calm. Quiet. Rugged.

I'll never forget what happened.

I turned to him, probably with panic all over my face, and asked: "What do you think we should do?"

Without a pause, without even the faintest flinch, he looked out into the swirling chaos and said:

**"I'm gonna use this as a tailwind to go faster."**

Wait, what?

Here I was, practically bracing for impact—and Ben saw an advantage.

He didn't just face the storm. He flipped it. In real time.

What most people would've labeled as dangerous, he saw as momentum. What I experienced as a problem, he experienced as possibility.

That single line changed me. I still think about it when life gets gusty.

"I'm gonna use this as a tailwind."

That's Face the Fear & Flip It in action. Not a bumper sticker. Not a Pinterest quote. A real, living, breathing moment in the middle of a lightning storm.

Fast forward to 2023—my third year on RAAM. I knew more now. I'd been through it. Grown from it. But this year tested all of us in new ways.

It was 2 AM. One of the last hard shifts. Raining. We were deep into the race. Running on grit, fumes, and sheer willpower. Everyone exhausted. The finish line near, but the physical and emotional toll peaking.

I was standing in the rain, again with the same teammate, Ben, only it was two years later and we were approaching the end of a grueling shift. That's when he looked at me and said:

"Rach, I'm tired."

Three simple words. But in RAAM, they're a red flag.

This isn't a race where people casually mention fatigue. Saying "I'm tired" isn't just a comment—it's a crack in the armor. A signal that someone is dangerously close to the edge.

And this wasn't just any rider. Days before, he'd needed multiple IV bags for dehydration. He'd climbed Wolf Creek Pass in Colorado—one of the most brutal sections of the race. He'd shown relentless grit, day and night.

So when he said those words, I knew he was near his limit.

We stood there together in the rain, waiting. Two uphill miles in the dark ahead of him. I tried to make him laugh, keep his energy up. I didn't try to fix it. I just stayed with him in it.

When his shift started, I racked the other racer's bike, climbed into the van, and immediately got on comms.

"He said he's tired. We need to dial in."

And we did. But not in the way you might think.

We didn't blast his favorite song. We didn't downplay what was ahead.

We knew this was the epitome of what RAAM does to your psyche. It was the whole point of the journey—to see how far you can go mentally, physically, emotionally.

We just held the space for him to do what he needed to do. To let the words "I'm tired" leave his mind and replace them with the strength and will he had created within himself during all those previous miles.

The follow vehicle stayed right behind him as we (the exchange van) leapfrogged ahead to track the miles. The road kept going up. The minutes ticked by. I'd occasionally try to make him laugh, not knowing what was going on between his ears. I knew it was a battle of him vs. himself, but wasn't sure who was winning.

Then something shifted.

We pulled over at the rider exchange point and spotted his headlamp coming. It didn't slow down.

Not only did he ride those last two miles, but he decided to keep going. He finished his shift and then rode past the handoff point. He just kept riding, something none of us could have anticipated.

That. Moment. Changed. Everything.

Not just for him—for all of us. Because we witnessed what happens when someone refuses to quit. When someone tells themself that they will keep pushing and FIO.

## The Pattern that Changes Everything:

Two different years. Two different moments of fear. But the same fundamental choice:

Will you let fear define the moment, or will you flip it into fuel?

Ben saw a terrifying storm and chose to see a tailwind. He faced those uphill miles and chose to keep pedaling past his exchange point.

He did what Path 3 people do—he flipped their fear in real time.

This isn't about being fearless. Ben probably felt the storm's danger and exhaustion. But he understood something crucial:

**Fear is information, not instruction.**

It tells you something important is happening. It doesn't tell you to stop.

One person's decision to keep going doesn't just move them forward. It strengthens the entire team. It lifts the people around them. It reminds everyone of what's possible.

Now, I know what you're thinking: "That's great, Rachel, but I'm not racing across America. How does this apply to my life?"

We all face our own version of that storm. Maybe it's a presentation you're dreading. A difficult conversation you need to have. A career change you've been putting off. A business you want to start but haven't.

The circumstances differ, but the fundamental challenge is the same: Will you face your fear and flip it into action, or will you let it stop you?

Sometimes Face the Fear and Flip It happens over hours in the rain with an exhausted cyclist. Sometimes it happens in seconds with no time to think.

**The phone call came at 10:45 PM**

I was laying with Hazel. Brad was somewhere over Texas, flying home from Dallas after a single meeting. The house was quiet.

"Mom?"

Olivia's voice. Already crying.

"Mom, we were mugged."

The tears made it hard to understand her at first.

"By machete. In the jungle."

My brain couldn't process those words mixed with her sobs. Machete. Jungle. I listened to my daughter crying from 2,400 miles away.

"We're okay. We're all okay. But Mom, they took everything."

She was trying to be brave through the tears, but I could hear the twenty-year-old who just needed her mom. The thieves took everything. Phones, Apple watches, wallets, IDs, backpacks— gone. The only things they didn't get? Their passports (miraculously left in the hotel safe) and just enough cash for Denny's that night.

Hours later, a small miracle: The police tracked Olivia's phone through Find My iPhone. Thankfully hers still had battery power. The thieves had dumped the phones after the mugging, probably once they realized they could be tracked.

"Mom, we have nothing. And we fly to Paraguay in two days."

More tears. Mine now too, but silent ones. She didn't need to hear my fear.

"Listen to me. I'm looking at flights right now. Right this second. I'll be there tomorrow."

I was already on my laptop while she cried. My fingers booking flights while my voice stayed steady for her.

"But Mom, you don't speak Spanish." Even in her time of struggle, she was worried about me.

"I'll figure it out. I'm coming."

The sound of her crying while I typed credit card numbers—
that's the sound of FIO when it matters most. When someone you
love is sobbing on the other side of the world, you don't think
about whether you're qualified to help. You just book the flight.

Brad was in the air. I texted him: "Call me as soon as you land."

From that moment, the timeline became a blur. Booking flights
while soothing her. Communicating with the girls' parents, Brad
landing, calling, me crying now. Wondering if he should come
too. Setting phone alarms every 30 minutes because I couldn't
risk oversleeping. I never went to bed. How could I? I could still
hear her crying.

Driving to the airport at 3 AM, having not slept, running on pure
adrenaline and a mother's love, I had perfect clarity:

I didn't speak Spanish—didn't matter.

I'd never been to Costa Rica—didn't matter.

I was exhausted—didn't matter.

I could still hear her crying. That's all that mattered.

Looking back now, after recognizing my FIO pattern, I realize
this was the fastest I've ever moved through the loop. The fear
was there—terror, actually—but her tears flipped everything
instantly. The fear of "machete, jungle, daughter" became fuel
for "get to Olivia now." Every minute from 10:45 PM to my 3
AM departure was action. Book flight while still on the phone.
Text Brad. Contact parents. Pack minimal. Screenshot
everything.

Fifteen hours from call to arrival. No sleep. No Spanish. No plan
beyond "get to Olivia."

Standing at the San José airport ATMs, calculating how much three college girls need for two months in Paraguay, I was still fueled by her tears. Photos became my language—hotel address screenshot meant "take me here," the calculator app meant "how much?" It turns out you can navigate a foreign country on no sleep with iPhone photos, determination and sheer grit.

When I walked into that hotel lobby and saw three scared young women, I was overwhelmed with relief and could finally exhale.

## Why do I share these stories with you?

This story taught me something crucial about the FIO Loop. Speed is variable—Jesse Itzler took 2 hours 53 minutes, Costa Rica took 15 hours of non-stop action. But the pattern never changes. Face it, act immediately, figure it out as you go. And sometimes, when your daughter is crying from 2,400 miles away, you don't even notice you're doing it. You just move.

The sound of your child crying from another country doesn't leave room for hesitation. This was my fastest FIO ever because tears don't wait for you to feel ready. Love makes you FIO faster than fear can stop you.

Your version is coming. That call with tears—yours, theirs, both. That moment when someone you love is crying and you're too far away but you go anyway. When it comes, you'll discover what I did: when someone needs you that badly, FIO isn't even a choice. It's just what love does.

You just go. Through your own tears if necessary.

You just go.

Less than Fifteen hours from tears to reunion. That's Face the Fear and Flip It.  When there is no other choice, when love overrides everything else. Sometimes the flip isn't about positive thinking—it's about having something more important than fear.

But not every fear flip happens in crisis.

"Do one thing every day that scares you."

—Eleanor Roosevelt

## The Everyday Fear Flip

Think about the last time you hesitated to take action on something important. Maybe it was:

- Starting a side business
- Having a difficult conversation
- Applying for a promotion
- Making a significant life change
- Trying something new and unfamiliar

Whatever the situation, your brain likely generated a series of "what if" scenarios:

"What if I fail?" "What if I'm rejected?" "What if I'm not ready?" "What if I make the wrong decision?"

These thoughts feel protective, but they keep us stuck, waiting for certainty that never arrives.

The first step of the FIO Loop—Face the Fear & Flip It—gives you a systematic way to move through this hesitation instead of being paralyzed by it.

When I decided to pitch Jesse Itzler about bringing Hell on the Hill to Maine, all those same fears surfaced. Who was I to approach someone of his stature? What if he dismissed the idea immediately? What if I looked foolish?

I could have talked myself out of it. Instead, I applied the first step of the FIO Loop.

I faced the fear directly—acknowledging it rather than suppressing it.

Then I flipped it: "What if he loves this idea?" "What if this is exactly the kind of fresh approach he's looking for?" "What if this becomes a significant opportunity for both of us?"

This mental flip didn't eliminate uncertainty. It didn't guarantee success. But it created enough space from fear for possibility to emerge.

## Why Your Brain Defaults to Fear (and how to change it)

Remember your brain wasn't designed for happiness or fulfillment—it was designed for survival. And from a survival perspective, avoidance of risk makes perfect sense. Our ancestors who were cautious lived longer than those who weren't.

This means your brain's default setting is to scan for threats, anticipate problems, and keep you safely within your comfort zone. It's not a design flaw—it's a feature that kept our species alive.

The problem? Modern life rarely presents the physical dangers our brains evolved to avoid. Instead, the threats we face are psychological—rejection, failure, embarrassment, uncertainty.

### The Fear Circuit

Neuroscientists have mapped what happens in your brain when fear takes hold:

Your amygdala—the brain's threat detection center—activates first, often before your conscious mind even registers why. This triggers a cascade of stress hormones including cortisol and adrenaline.

These hormones prepare your body for fight-or-flight: heart rate increases, breathing accelerates, blood rushes to major muscle groups.

Simultaneously, activity in your prefrontal cortex—responsible for rational thinking and decision-making—decreases, making it harder to think clearly.

This explains why fear feels so overwhelming and why "just think positive" rarely works in the moment. Your brain is literally shifting resources away from rational thought toward survival functions.

But here's the good news: this circuit can be rewired through deliberate practice and repeated exposure to what you fear.

When you flip your fear, you're not ignoring it or suppressing it. You're working with your brain's natural wiring to create a different outcome.

Imagine you need to have a difficult conversation—maybe asking for a raise, addressing a problem with a colleague, or setting a boundary.

Your brain's fear circuit immediately activates: "They'll get defensive." "It will damage the relationship." "I'll mess it up and make things worse."

These thoughts feel real and predictive. But they're not facts—they're just your brain's automatic threat assessment.

The flip doesn't deny the possibility of challenges. Instead, it introduces equally valid positive possibilities: "This could lead to better understanding between us." "They might appreciate my honesty." "This could strengthen our relationship in the long run."

This mental flip doesn't guarantee a perfect outcome. But it creates enough space from fear for possibility to emerge.

In my Boston Marathon experience, this moment came after months of doubt. I wasn't a runner. I'd barely run more than a few miles at a stretch. The idea of completing 26.2 miles seemed next to impossible.

As the race approached, fear flooded my system: "I'm afraid I won't be able to finish." "I'm afraid I'll embarrass myself." "I'm afraid I'll be exposed as someone who doesn't belong there."

The flip came when I considered alternative possibilities: "What if I surprise myself with what I'm capable of?" "What if the energy of the event carries me through?" "What if completing this, regardless of time, becomes one of my proudest achievements?"

This mental shift created a crucial opening—a moment where something other than fear could guide my decisions.

## The Launching Belief in Action

Remember from Chapter 1: The FIO Mindset is powered by Launching Beliefs—the commitment to figure it out rather than the confidence you already know how.

What makes a Launching Belief different? It's not based on confidence. It's based on commitment. You don't need to believe you'll succeed—you just need to believe you'll figure it out.

When Ben looked at that storm, he didn't have confidence the tailwind would work perfectly. He had a launching belief that he'd figure out how to use it.

When I pitched Jesse Itzler, I didn't have confidence that he would say yes. I had a launching belief that regardless of the outcome, I would find a way to make something positive happen.

This distinction is crucial because it liberates you from needing to feel confident before you act. It gives you permission to move forward even when the path is unclear.

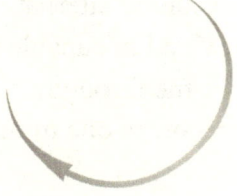

# THE FLIP IT FORMULA

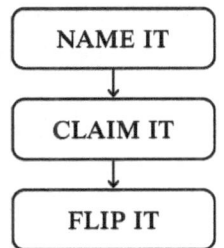

Let's break down exactly how to master the first step of the FIO Loop:

## 1. NAME IT - Identify Your Specific Fear

This isn't about vague anxiety, but pinpointing exactly what you're afraid might happen. Write it down. Make it concrete. "I'm afraid that ____."

## 2. CLAIM IT - Take Ownership of the Fear

Recognize that fear is information, not a command. It's a natural response, not a character flaw. "I notice I'm feeling afraid about ____."

## 3. FLIP IT - Consider the Opposite Possibility

For every negative "what if," propose a positive "what if." "What if, instead of ____, the result is ____?"

This creates the opening—the possibility—that makes everything else possible.

Remember Ben's flip: He didn't deny the storm was dangerous. He just asked a different question: "What if this helps me go faster?"

That's the power of the flip. It's not about pretending everything will be perfect. It's about recognizing that your brain's first draft—the disaster scenario—is just one possibility among many.

## The Worry Calibration: I Worry If I Have To

I want to share something I've learned along the way that has completely shifted my anxiety:

**I worry only if I have to.**

Not "I don't worry." I worry IF I HAVE TO. Because we're human. We're literally programmed for survival—it's in our DNA. Our ancestors survived because they worried about rustling bushes and strange sounds. Regardless of how far we are out of the cave, that wiring doesn't just disappear.

But here's what research shows: The things we worry about almost never happen the way we imagine them.

Studies from Cornell University found that 85% of what people worried about never happened at all. And of the 15% that did happen, 79% of people said they handled it better than expected or learned a valuable lesson. That means 97% of our worry is wasted energy on catastrophes that either never arrive or become opportunities for growth.

We catastrophize because our brains can't tell the difference between a charging bear and a challenging email. Same alarm system. Same stress response. Same "what if everything goes wrong" spiral.

But when you've been through enough life, you learn to calibrate your worry meter:

- Will this matter in 5 years? Probably not worth the worry.
- Can I influence the outcome? Maybe worth some strategic thinking.
- Is this a pattern or a one-time thing? Patterns deserve attention.
- Am I adding suffering to a situation that already has enough? Stop it.

My practice is simple: See things as they are, not worse than they are.

That presentation you're dreading? Your brain is showing you public humiliation. Reality will probably be a few fumbled words and people checking their phones.

That conversation you're avoiding? Your brain is scripting relationship-ending drama. Reality will probably be awkward for five minutes then relief.

That business risk? Your brain is calculating bankruptcy. Reality will probably be learning what works and what doesn't.

After losing my mom at six and my dad decades later, after microbursts and muggings and failed attempts, I've learned that the catastrophes we imagine are almost always worse than what actually happens. And even when the worst does happen, we figure it out. We survive. We FIO.

So yes, I worry if I have to. But I've learned to check:

Do I actually have to? Is this worth my limited worry budget? Or is my DNA just doing that thing where it treats everyday challenges like saber-toothed tigers?

Usually, it's the tiger thing.

This isn't about being fearless. It's about being selective with your fear. It's about knowing that 97% of what you're worried about right now will either never happen or become a story about how you figured it out.

Mark Twain said it best: "I've had a lot of worries in my life, most of which never happened."

So when fear shows up, I ask myself: Is this something I need to worry about, or just something to figure out?

The answer is almost always: Just figure it out.

Because our brains are wired for survival, but we're living in a world where most "threats" are just opportunities wearing scary masks. Once you see that, once you realize the anxiety you're carrying is about things that statistically won't happen, you can put that energy into action instead.

Worry if you have to. But check if you actually have to. Chances are, you don't.

"The thing you fear most has no power. Your fear of it is what has the power."

— Oprah Winfrey

## The Optimism Edge: My Operating System

At the heart of the fear flip is strategic optimism—the belief that while challenges are real, so is your ability to overcome them.

Let me be clear: I'm not talking about toxic positivity or pretending everything is fine when it's not. I'm talking about the kind of optimism that sees a microburst destroy your triathlon and thinks, "Well, now we have a legendary story." The kind that loses your mom at six and decides to focus on the love you got to experience rather than the years you lost. The kind that runs the Boston Marathon with lingering bronchitis and thinks, "At least I'll never wonder what if."

This isn't natural for everyone. But for me? Optimism isn't just how I think—it's how I survive.

Research from the University of Pennsylvania found that optimists aren't people who never face setbacks. They're people who explain setbacks differently. When something goes wrong, they see it as:

- Temporary rather than permanent
- Specific rather than universal
- Surmountable rather than defining

Here's how this plays out in real life:

**When I got rejected from TEDx (three times):**

- Pessimist: "I'm not good enough. I'll never get picked for anything."
- Me: "My talk wasn't right for this specific event. I'll refine it and try again. Fourth time's the charm, right?"

**When my daughter called crying from Costa Rica:**

- Pessimist: "This is a disaster. She never should have gone."
- Me: "This is a problem with a solution. She's safe, I can get there, we'll figure it out."

This explanatory style—how you explain events to yourself— shapes whether you face challenges with hope or helplessness.

But here's what nobody tells you about optimism: It's not about being happy when things go wrong. It's about believing you can influence what happens next. When life handed me loss after loss—my mom, then my dad—I had two choices: Let grief define my boundaries or let love define my actions. I chose love I chose to see every day as borrowed time to make impact.

My friends joke that I could find the silver lining in a tornado. They're not wrong. But it's not because I'm naturally sunny—it's because I've trained myself to ask different questions:

Instead of "Why me?" I ask "What can I learn?"

Instead of "What if I fail?" I ask "What if this works?"

Instead of "This is terrible" I ask "Where's the opportunity?"

This isn't denial. It's strategic. Because while I'm looking for the lesson or the silver lining, I'm not paralyzed. I'm moving. I'm figuring it out. My optimism isn't passive. It's fuel.

When you flip your fear from "What if I fail?" to "What if I succeed?", you're not just changing a thought.

**You're changing your entire operating system from one that protects to one that propels.**

Strategic optimism fuels launching beliefs by focusing not on guaranteed success, but on guaranteed learning and adaptation. Every outcome has value. Every attempt builds data. Every fear faced makes the next one smaller.

The truth? Optimism isn't about believing everything will work out perfectly. It's about believing YOU will work it out, regardless. It's about knowing that even if you fail, you'll extract the lesson, find the gift, and use it to fuel your next attempt.

That's not just positive thinking. That's the foundation of FIO.

Because here's what years of directing races taught me: The runners who finish aren't the ones who never doubt. They're the ones who reframe their doubt as data. Who see hills as opportunities to get stronger. Who treat mile 20 not as "I have 6 miles left" but as "I've already conquered 20."

Same race. Same hills. Same distance. Different story.

Your brain believes the story you tell it. So why not tell it one where you're the hero who figures it out?

That's the optimism edge. Not pretending challenges don't exist, but believing (and knowing) that you're resourceful enough to handle them.

And if you can't believe it yet? Borrow mine. I've got plenty to share.

Because I've learned that optimism, like courage, is contagious. When one person flips their fear and finds the opportunity, everyone around them starts looking for it too.

## When FIO Builds Bridges

Some of the most meaningful things in my life exist because I didn't listen to fear.

In 2017, South Berwick, Maine—a predominantly white New England town of 7,500—decided to become sister cities with Tuskegee, Alabama, home to the Tuskegee Airmen and ground zero for civil rights history. Most people thought bridging these communities was impossible.

When they announced they were forming a committee, every logical voice in my head protested: "You don't know anything about sister cities." "You've never done community bridge-building." "Stick to races and events—that's what you know."

Those voices weren't wrong. I had zero qualifications. No relevant experience.

But something deeper whispered: "What if this is exactly where you should be?"

So I joined. I showed up and figured it out as I went—same way I FIO everything.

December 3, 2017. Our first delegation trip to Tuskegee. The schedule was insane—if you had 10 seconds to breathe, you were probably running late. We flew into Atlanta, drove 90 minutes to Tuskegee, had lunch with the mayor, toured the university, and ended our first day at their annual Christmas concert.

That evening, in a beautifully decorated church, I found myself sitting behind 87-year-old Antoinette Frederick. When the choir director invited the audience to join the "Hallelujah Chorus," she turned to me.

"Will you help me up the stairs and join me?"

My first thought: *I can't sing.* My second: *Please don't let this involve solos.*

But I couldn't say no to her warmth.

Standing on that stage, no idea if I was in the right section or even in tune, I understood something profound. Antoinette wasn't just inviting me to sing—she was building a bridge one gesture at a time. Showing me how community happens: through invitation, through vulnerability, through showing up even when you don't know the words.

Later that night, Mayor Tony Haygood said something that stopped me cold:

"Progress is like a train. People will hop on and off, but the train rolls on. It's our job to keep it going."

That first trip, our delegation navigated everything:

- Conversations about race and history we'd never had before
- Sharing meals and stories
- Learning their traditions while sharing ours
- Building trust one interaction at a time

The next year, they came to Maine—experiencing lobster, lighthouses, and the cold Atlantic. Then we went back. Then they came again. Trip after trip, conversation after conversation, meal after meal. We figured out how to bridge misunderstandings, different perspectives on history, centuries of division.

I even tried (and failed spectacularly) to make my Tuskegee friend Pam's fried chicken recipe. My kitchen became a disaster zone, but my attempt to cook southern fried chicken created a story we still laugh about today. We marched together across the

Edmund Pettus Bridge, feeling the weight of history under our feet. We've cried together over losses, celebrated victories.

Fast forward to today, our students connect through virtual exchanges. Our historians teach in each other's schools. What started as formal delegations became friends texting about kids. South Berwick doesn't just have a sister city—we have family. Our town council even declared June 22 as "Tuskegee Day."

Two vastly different communities, 1,300 miles apart, connected by a common desire for progress, because a group of people decided to hop on Mayor Tony's train of progress.

Sometimes FIO means stepping into spaces where you don't know the rules. Sometimes it means singing the "Hallelujah Chorus" when you barely know the tune.

That night on stage, singing badly but singing anyway, was just another FIO moment. Another fear faced and flipped. Another piece of evidence that when you say yes to the invitation—even when you don't know the words—something beautiful happens.

The Common Ground Sister City Project again reaffirmed for me that FIO works everywhere—in business, in races, in communities, in relationships. Any challenge can start to be figured out with one conversation, one meal, and even one failed fried chicken recipe at a time.

## CHAPTER 4 TAKEAWAYS

The first step of the FIO Loop—Face the Fear and Flip It—isn t just a technique. It's the doorway through which all meaningful change must pass.

Fear speaks first, and it speaks loudest. But remember fear is information, not instruction. It's your brain's warning system, not your navigation system. The difference between those who move and those who remain frozen isn't the absence of fear—it's understanding that fear is data to be considered, not simply commands to be obeyed.

Your brain evolved to keep you alive, not to make you happy. It will always emphasize threats over opportunities, dangers over possibilities. The flip doesn't deny the threats—it restores balance by illuminating what else might be true.

This is where the FIO Mindset separates itself from everything else you've tried. You don't need confidence—that's the lie that keeps people waiting forever. You need what I call Launching Beliefs: the commitment to figure it out as you go rather than the certainty that you already know how. It's the difference between waiting for courage and choosing to be courageous.

Remember Ben in that storm, staring at chaos and saying, "I'm gonna use this as a tailwind." He didn't eliminate the danger. He didn't pretend the storm wasn't real. He flipped his relationship to it. Sometimes the thing that scares you most is exactly what will propel you forward—but only if you flip it from obstacle to opportunity.

And here's what I've learned from every stage, every starting line, every committee I had no business joining: Courage is contagious. Your decision to keep going doesn't just change you. It lifts everyone around you. It gives others permission to flip their own fears. One person's FIO has the power to become someone else's possibility.

## YOUR CHAPTER 4 ACTION

Right now, there's a storm in your life. Maybe it's been building for months. Maybe it arrived this morning. Either way, you have Ben's choice: Let it stop you or use it as a tailwind.

The Flip Formula in action:

Name it: What exactly are you afraid might happen?

_____

Not vague anxiety. Specific fear. Write it down.

Claim it: This fear is information about what matters to you. What is it protecting? What does it reveal about what you value?

_____

Flip it: If the opposite happened, if it went impossibly well, what might that look like? _____

Now ask yourself Ben's question: "How could I use this as a tailwind?"

What force in this fear could actually push you forward?

_____

The crucial final step: What's one tiny action you could take in the next hour?

_____

This flip creates the opening. But without action, it's just positive thinking. With action—even the tiniest step—it becomes transformation.

Set a timer for one hour. When it goes off, that tiny action had better be done.

---

You don't need to feel ready. You don't need confidence. You just need a launching belief—the commitment that whatever happens, you'll figure out the next step.

The fear you're facing isn't your enemy. It's your intelligence system showing you where your growth lives. On the other side of that fear is the person you're becoming.

Turn the page. Let me show you why identifying one action—not ten, not the perfect one, just one—is the secret to making the flip real.

"I have been impressed with the urgency of doing. Knowing is not enough;

we must apply.

Being willing is not enough; we must do."

— Leonardo da Vinci

# 5

# Identify One Action

"Never leave the site of a goal without taking action toward it."

— Tony Robbins

My husband Brad has had a one-hour commute both ways for the majority of his professional career. In the beginning he started listening to personal growth and development CD's to take advantage of the time in the car.

One day I was taking advantage of his collection and started listening to the "Goal Setting Workshop" portion of one of Tony Robbins' CD's. It was during this lesson I heard a line that helped change the trajectory of everything I have done since:

**"Never leave the sight of a goal without taking some sort of action towards it."**

This one sentence changed how I approach literally everything.

It's not about the perfect action. It's not about strategic action. It's about **ANY** action, taken immediately, that moves you toward what you want.

Here's what Tony understood that most people don't:

**The moment you set a goal, identify a dream, or flip a fear, you're standing at a crossroads. One path leads to transformation. The other leads back to who you've always been.**

The only difference between those paths? Whether you take action before you leave that moment.

## The PTO Permission Slip

My son Ethan was in kindergarten, and we were just hanging out one afternoon listening to Wayne from Maine. Wayne was the local children's musician who was basically the Beatles for the under-10 crowd in our area.

As Wayne sang about lobsters and blueberries and moose (because Maine), an idea popped into my head: "What if Wayne performed at Central Elementary, at the end of the school year"? We could create a celebration for all the kids who made it through another year.

I could see it perfectly; Wayne on the stage out in front of Central Elementary School. I could clearly picture 300 kids losing their minds, teachers finally relaxing, parents taking pictures. We could call it "Central Celebrations".

Most people would have thought "cute idea" and gone back to folding laundry. But I'd learned something from Tony Robbins: Never leave the site of a goal without taking action toward it.

So right there, with Wayne still singing "Clark, Clark the Toothless Shark" in the background, I grabbed a piece of paper and wrote: "Central Celebrations - Wayne from Maine - End of school year."

That was action one. The idea now existed outside my head.

## The PTO Ambush

Three days later, I'm at a PTO meeting. I was a new member and didn't have any experience with the group yet. During "new business," my hand shot up.

"Hey, wouldn't it be cool if we had an end-of-year celebration with Wayne from Maine performing for the kids? We could call it Central Celebrations."

The PTO president barely looked up from her notes. "Sure, if you can find a sponsor and make it happen, go for it."

Now, most people hear that as "Good luck with that impossible task."

I heard "YES!"

I also heard a challenge. And, just in case you haven't figured this out yet- I don't back down from challenges.

Remember Tony's principle? Never leave the site of a goal without action? Well, I didn't even leave the BUILDING after that PTO meeting without taking the next action.

I made a list of all of the business owners I knew in town. The very next day, I walked into my friends business in town.

"Want to sponsor something amazing for kids?" I asked, still high on PTO adrenaline.

"What is it?"

"Wayne from Maine performing for the whole school at the end of the year!

"Sure."

Done. Sponsor secured. Total time from PTO "permission" to sponsorship: less than 24 hours.

## The House Party Bonus

Here's where I had the opportunity to build on momentum: When I called Wayne's booking person to set up Central Celebrations, I had a thought: "Do you guys do house parties too?"

Turns out, yes, yes they do.

And that is how Wayne from Maine ended up performing at my son Ethan's birthday party the following year.

## The Twenty-Year Echo

Central Celebrations? It ran for YEARS. It became a tradition. Kids who went through Central school are now in their twenties, and they still remember Wayne from Maine closing out their elementary school years.

And here's the thing that kills me: I almost didn't raise my hand at that PTO meeting. I almost waited for someone else to suggest it. I almost let "someday-itis" win.

But twenty years later, I can tell you exactly what those first actions created:

- Thousands of kids with a core memory
- A school tradition that lasted over a decade
- The confidence to ask for bigger things
- The knowledge that "Sure, if you can make it happen" really means go make it happen.

That was twenty years ago. Ethan's 26 now. And every impossible thing I've done since then—including getting another famous musician to play in our backyard—started with the confidence I built from Wayne from Maine.

Because here's what I learned: Once you prove to yourself that children's musicians will play your events, even more famous ones don't seem that impossible anymore.

## From Crazy Idea to Annual Tradition

Brad's 40th birthday was coming up, and I had a crazy thought: What if his favorite musician performed at his party?

Not a cover band. Not a DJ playing Pat McGee Band songs. The. Actual. Artist. Pat McGee.

Most people would have had that thought and immediately talked themselves out of it. "That's ridiculous." "He's a touring musician." "That would cost a fortune." "Who am I to even ask?"

But I'd been living by Tony Robbins' rule for years: Never leave the site of a goal without taking action toward it.

So right there, standing in my kitchen with this insane idea, I opened my laptop.

**First action:** Google "Pat McGee Band tour schedule." I scanned the dates around Brad's birthday. Nothing. The band's calendar was empty for that weekend.

**Second action:** Find his booking contact. This took approximately three minutes. It was right there on his website.

**Third action:** Send the email before my brain could stop me.

"Hi, I'm planning my husband's 40th birthday party in Maine. He's a huge fan. Do you do private events?" There was more in there, but you get the idea.

Click and send.

The whole thing took less than ten minutes from crazy idea to email sent. Classic FIO—I didn't know HOW to book a rock star for a house party. I just figured I'd figure it out.

He responded quite quickly, but the cost for the whole band wasn't in the price range. I responded asking what it would cost for just him to come and play. He replied back that he would have to come with the other Pat, Pat McAloon, and they could do an acoustic set.

That new cost worked for me…I could ask people to chuck in a few bucks at the party in lieu of cards and silly 40th gifts that no-one really needs anyhow.  I sent the deposit before I could second-guess myself.

The night of Brad's party, everyone was there—friends, family, neighbors. Brad had no idea that I had booked the two Pat's for an acoustic set.  He thought it was just a regular backyard birthday party and he would be jamming with just his own band, PB&J.  Everyone at the party knew but him that his favorite musicians would be coming to his party.

I had timed it just right so that PB&J would be playing one of McGee's songs when the two Pat's walked through the backyard to surprise Brad.

As the two Pat's walked through the house, and onto the back deck to where Brad and the boys were playing the crowd cleared a path.  Brad's face went through about seventeen different emotions in just about three seconds. Confusion. Recognition. Disbelief. Pure joy.  The Pat's walked up to where the guys were playing and finished singing the song with them.  It was one of those unforgettable memories none of us will ever forget.

A wife of the year award goes to….me.

But here's where the story gets better:

Pat told us that he had such a good time.  The intimate setting, the genuine fans, the authentic connection.  When he was leaving, he signed one of his posters for Brad with the inscription reading: "To the Martins- please adopt us!"

That was ten years ago.

Since then, Pat McGee has come back almost every summer.  He even came back this year to help us celebrate Brad's 50th. A couple of summers ago the WHOLE BAND came for our daughter's Jack and Jill pre-wedding shower. The. Entire. Pat McGee Band, in our backyard. For a wedding shower.

What started as a "crazy" 40th birthday idea has become something none of us could have imagined. Our friends mark their calendars a year in advance. People plan vacations around it. It's become legendary in our circle, when spring rolls around, we are asked: "When are the Pat's coming this summer?"

## The Compound Effect of One Email

That ten-minute action—sending one email I "had no business" sending—created:

- A decade of unforgettable memories
- Brad sharing his 40th AND 50th birthdays with his favorite musician
- Our daughter's pre-wedding celebration with the full band
- A genuine friendship with artists we admire
- Annual gatherings that bring our community together
- Proof that "impossible" is just an opinion

But it only happened because I didn't wait to figure out the perfect approach. I didn't research "how to book musicians for private parties." I didn't form a committee or create a spreadsheet or wait until I felt "ready" to reach out to a famous musician.

I had the thought. I took the action. I figured it out as I went.

**Never leave the site of a goal without taking action toward it.**

### The Evolution of Impossible

If someone had told me when I sent that first email that the Pat McGee Band would play my daughter's wedding shower in my backyard, I would have said they were insane.

But that's how FIO works. You don't see the whole staircase. You just take the first step.

- Year 1: "Can Pat play Brad's birthday?" → He does
- Year 2: "Want to come back?" → He does
- Year 7: "Could the whole band come?" → They do
- Year 10: "Still happening!" → Brad's 50th with Pat and this time he even brought Silent Disco with him!

Each impossibility became the new normal, which made the next impossibility seem possible.

### The Truth About "Crazy" Ideas

Your "crazy" ideas aren't crazy. They're just untested.

Pat McGee doesn't play house parties for everyone. But he plays ours because ten years ago, I took ten minutes to figure it out instead of spending ten years wishing I had.

Your equivalent of Pat McGee is out there. That "impossible" thing you want? It's probably one email away. One phone call. One action you can take in the next ten minutes.

*The question isn't whether it's possible. The question is whether you are willing to take the first action to find out.*

Even if that action is googling "how to book a rock star for a birthday party."

Especially then. Because your version of Pat McGee—that impossible thing that would change everything—is waiting for you to stop thinking and start googling.

That ten-minute email to Pat McGee taught me something I'd use again and again: The "impossible" people—the ones you think would never respond, never say yes, never show up—they're

152

often the most likely to surprise you. They got where they are by saying yes to unexpected opportunities. By seeing possibilities where others see boundaries.

## Why this Works: The Neuroscience of Now

When you set a goal or make a decision, your brain opens what neuroscientists call a "motivation window."

For a brief moment—usually minutes, sometimes hours—your prefrontal cortex (decision center) and your motor cortex (action center) are perfectly aligned. The path from thought to action is clear.

But that window doesn't stay open.

Take action in that window, and your brain strengthens the neural pathway from intention to action. Your identity shifts: "I'm someone who does things."

Miss that window, and your brain strengthens a different pathway—from intention to hesitation. Your identity reinforces: "I'm someone who thinks about things."

This is why Tony's principle is genius. It's not motivational fluff. It's brain science.

The action doesn't have to be big. It just has to happen while the window is open.

## The Compound Effect of Immediate Action

Here's what happens when you never leave the site of a goal without taking action:

**Day 1:** You take one small action. Your brain notices.

**Week 1:** You've taken seven actions. Your brain starts building a pattern.

**Month 1:** You've taken 30 actions. Your identity is shifting.

**Year 1:** You've taken 365 actions. You're unrecognizable.

Every action is a vote for who you're becoming. Every time you leave the site of a goal WITH action, you vote for "I'm someone who makes things happen."

Every time you leave WITHOUT action, you vote for "I'm someone who only dreams about things."

The compound effect isn't just about results. It's about identity.

**The Lie that Keeps you Stuck**

"I'll take action when I'm ready."

This is the biggest lie we tell ourselves. Because "ready" is not a feeling that comes before action. It's a feeling that comes FROM action.

I wasn't ready to pitch Jesse. The action of googling how to pitch him made me ready.

I wasn't ready to run a marathon. The action of paying the deposit made me ready.

Ready follows action. Always.

Think about it: How do you get ready to swim? By getting in the water. How do you get ready to speak publicly? By speaking publicly. How do you get ready to start a business? By starting.

The preparation paradox is this: The only way to feel ready is to start before you feel ready.

## Your Two-Minute Window

Here's my rule, inspired by Tony's principle: If it takes less than two minutes, do it now.

You know what takes less than two minutes?

- Sending the text that starts the conversation
- Making the call that opens the door
- Registering for the thing that scares you
- Booking the flight that commits you
- Creating the document that begins the project
- Posting the announcement that creates accountability
- Buying the domain that claims your idea
- Scheduling the meeting that forces preparation
- Sending the email that requests the opportunity

Two minutes. That's all that stands between your current life and your next level.

But here's the thing most people don't realize: Those two minutes are MORE powerful than two hours of planning. Because those two minutes change your identity from thinker to doer.

## THE IDENTITY SHIFT FORMULA

When you take immediate action, here's what actually happens:

**Before action:** "I'm someone who wants to write a book."

**After writing one page:** "I'm someone who's writing a book."

**Before action:** "I'm someone who should exercise."

**After one walk:** "I'm someone who exercises."

**Before action:** "I'm someone who dreams of starting a business."

**After buying the domain:** "I'm someone who's building a business."

The action doesn't have to complete the goal. It just has to start the identity shift.

## The Emergency Protocol

Sometimes you're frozen. The goal is clear but the action isn't. Here's your emergency protocol:

Ask yourself: "What's the smallest thing I could do right now that would make backing out harder?"

For Boston, it was paying the deposit. Once money was spent, backing out meant losing it.

For Jesse, it was sending the DM. Once sent, the conversation was started.

For Rick's Run, it was choosing the date and committing to the timing company.

The best first actions create commitment. They burn boats. They make retreat uncomfortable.

## What Immediate Action Really Means

Immediate doesn't mean "later today." Immediate doesn't mean "after coffee." Immediate doesn't mean "when I get home."

Immediate means NOW. Before you do anything else. Before your brain can generate excuses.

When I heard Tony say those words on that CD, I pressed pause and took action on something I'd been thinking about for months.

Didn't finish the CD first. Didn't wait until the lesson was complete.

Never. Leave. The. Site.

This is the difference between Path 2 people (eternal preparation) and Path 3 people (immediate action). Path 2 people leave the site to "think about it more." Path 3 people take action before they leave.

### The Evidence Collection System

Every immediate action you take becomes evidence of who you are:

Action 1: "I guess I'm someone who does things." Action 10: "I'm definitely someone who takes action." Action 50: "I'm known for getting things done."    Action 100: "This is just who I am."

Your brain collects this evidence and updates your identity accordingly. You don't have to believe you're an action-taker. You just have to act like one. The belief follows the evidence.

## YOUR TRANSFORMATION PROTOCOL

Right now—not when you finish this chapter—think of something you want.

Got it?

Now take one action toward it. Any action. The smallest action.

- Send the text
- Open the document
- Make the call
- Book the appointment
- Register for the thing
- Post the announcement

Do it now. Before you read another word.

I'm serious. Tony's principle only works if you use it. And the principle applies to the principle itself—don't leave the site of learning this principle without taking action on it.

Put the book down. Take one action. Then come back.

**Did you do it?**

If yes, you just proved you're someone who never leaves the site of a goal without taking action. You're becoming Path 3.

If not, you're treating transformation like information. You're still on Path 2, preparing to change instead of changing.

**The Ripple Effect**

When you never leave the site of a goal without taking action, something magical happens: Other people start doing it too.

Your kids see you take immediate action and learn that's how goals work.

Your team sees you move without hesitation and starts moving faster.

Your friends see you doing instead of discussing and start doing too.

You become a walking permission slip for others to stop waiting and start moving.

This is how movements start. Not with perfect plans. With immediate action that inspires more immediate action.

"The way to get started is to quit talking and begin doing."

—Walt Disney

## CHAPTER 5 TAKEAWAYS

- Never leave the site of a goal without taking action toward it—this is the difference between dreaming and doing
- The motivation window opens briefly when you set a goal—act before it closes
- Ready is not a prerequisite for action; it's a result of action
- Two-minute actions are more powerful than two-hour plans
- Every immediate action is a vote for who you're becoming
- The best first actions create commitment and make backing out harder
- Your brain collects evidence of your actions and updates your identity accordingly
- Path 3 people take action before they leave; Path 2 people leave to "think about it"

## YOUR FIO ACTION STEP

You know what to do. That thing you thought about while reading this chapter—take one action on it. Now. Not later. Not tomorrow. Now.

If you can't do the whole thing, do the first 2 minutes of it. If you can't do 2 minutes, do 30 seconds. If you can't do 30 seconds, send one text about it.

But whatever you do, don't leave this chapter without taking action.

Because that's the difference between reading about transformation and transforming.

Never leave the site of a goal without taking action toward it.

The site is here. The goal is clear. The time is now.

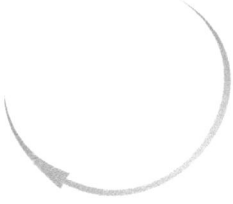

# 6

# Observe, Optimize & Celebrate - The Step That Turns Every Outcome Into Rocket Fuel

"What did you fail at this week?"

— The Blakely family dinner table question

## The Question That Built a Billionaire

Every week at dinner, Sara Blakely's dad asked his kids one question: "What did you fail at this week?"

Not "What went well?" Not "What did you achieve?" But "What did you fail at?"

If they didn't have an answer, he was disappointed. No failure meant no trying. No trying meant no growing.

When Sara failed—bombed a test, lost the game, got rejected—her dad would high-five her. "Way to go! What did you learn?"

This childhood ritual rewired Sara's brain. Failure became data. Rejection became research. Every "no" became information that got her closer to "yes."

That mindset helped her turn $5,000 and pantyhose into SPANX®, a billion-dollar company.

Her dad understood what most people don't: The outcome isn't the point. What you do with the outcome is everything.

Welcome to the most important step of the FIO Loop—the one that determines whether you'll quit or take that quantum leap.

## Why This Step Changes Everything

You sent the email. Made the call. Had the conversation. Took the leap.

The first two steps are done. You faced the fear, flipped it, identified one action, and took it.

Now reality responds. And this is where 90% of people quit.

Because when results don't match expectations (and they rarely do on the first try), most people conclude: "See? I knew this wouldn't work."

But FIO'ers know something different: The outcome is just data. And data is gold.

### The Three Outcomes (And Why They're All Wins)

After witnessing and living through hundreds of my own loops, every outcome falls into one of three categories:

### 1. THE "HECK YEAH!" OUTCOME

Everything worked better than expected. The email got an instant yes. The conversation went perfectly. The risk paid off immediately.

**What to Observe:** What specifically worked? What conditions were present?

**How to Optimize:** How can you scale this? What's the next level?

**What to Celebrate:** Everything! The action, outcome, and evidence that FIO works.

When Pat McGee said yes to Brad's birthday party, that was a Heck Yeah. But I still had to observe (he liked intimate venues), optimize (invite him back annually), and celebrate (we'd done the "impossible").

Real-Life Heck Yeah Examples:

- Asked for a raise → Got 20% instead of the 10% you expected
- Applied to one dream job → Got an interview within 24 hours
- Posted your art online → First piece sold within an hour
- Signed up for 5K → Discover you love running and want to do more

## 2. THE "MIXED BAG" OUTCOME

Some things worked, others didn't. You got a response but not the one you wanted.

**What to Observe:** What worked? What didn't? What surprised you?

**How to Optimize:** Keep what worked, adjust what didn't.

**What to Celebrate:** You got data! You're in the game!

Jesse's initial response was a mixed bag: "Amazing. I'll circle back post holiday!!!!!" Interested but not committed. Most people would have stopped there. I observed (he's interested but busy), optimized (create more value while waiting), and celebrated (I got a response from Jesse Itzler!).

**Real-Life Mixed Bag Examples:**

- Asked for a raise → No raise but got a title change and future review
- Applied to dream job → Rejection but personalized feedback on skills to develop
- Posted your art online → No sales but gained fifty followers who love your style
- Signed up for 5K → Struggled to finish but completed it walking

### 3. THE "WELL, THAT HAPPENED" OUTCOME

Complete disaster. Clear rejection. Obvious failure.

**What to Observe:** What specific factors contributed? What assumptions were wrong?

**How to Optimize:** Complete pivot needed or small adjustment?

**What to Celebrate:** You tried! You eliminated what doesn't work!

## Real-Life Well That Happened Examples:

- Asked for a raise → Boss says company is actually doing layoffs
- Applied to dream job → Auto-rejection email in 2 hours
- Posted your art online → Accidentally deleted your account while posting
- Signed up for 5K → Injured yourself training, can't participate

## The Hidden Gold in "Failures"

Here's what most people miss: "Well, That Happened" outcomes often teach you MORE than successes.

- Raise rejection → Learned company is struggling (time to job search)
- Job auto-rejection → Resume needs work (now you know)
- Deleted account → Forced to learn platform properly (become expert)
- Race injury → Body needs different training (prevent future injuries)

Every outcome contains data. Every data point gets you closer to success.

## Your Turn: Practice the Protocol

Think of your last "failure." Run it through:

OBSERVE: What actually happened? (Just facts) OPTIMIZE: What would you do differently? CELEBRATE: What took courage?

Then identify your next action based on this data.

## Breaking Down the "O": Your Three-Part Gold Mining Process

The third step of the FIO Loop isn't one action—it's three distinct parts that work together. Miss any one and you lose the power:

OBSERVE: Strip Away the Story

Just facts. No drama. No interpretation.

- Not "I totally bombed" → "They said no"
- Not "It was a disaster" → "Three things didn't work"
- Not "I crushed it" → "Got a yes in 24 hours"
- Not "Everyone hated it" → "Two people gave critical feedback"

You're a scientist recording data, not a novelist writing tragedy. Facts are useful. Stories keep you stuck.

**OPTIMIZE:** Make One Strategic Adjustment

Based on what you observed, what's ONE thing you'll change?

- If it worked → How can I repeat or scale this?
- If it partially worked → What do I keep? What do I adjust?
- If it failed → Do I need a complete pivot or just a tweak?

One specific change. Not "do better next time." Not a complete overhaul. One clear adjustment.

**CELEBRATE:** Complete the Neural Loop

This isn't optional. This is brain science.

- Celebrate the ACTION (you tried!)
- Celebrate the DATA (you learned!)
- Celebrate the COURAGE (you faced fear!)

Even 2 seconds counts. Fist pump. Say "I did it" out loud. Text yourself a trophy emoji. Your brain needs the dopamine hit to want to try again.

## The Three Questions That Change Everything

After mastering the basic Observe-Optimize-Celebrate, add these three questions that transform any experience into wisdom:

1. How did this happen FOR me? (Not TO me)

2. What did this teach me?

3. How will I use this in my next step?

These aren't feel-good questions. They're strategic extraction tools.

**When Jesse's response was "I'll circle back":**

1. **FOR me:** This happened FOR me to learn patience while maintaining momentum
2. **Taught me:** Interest doesn't mean immediate yes - nurture the connection
3. **Next step:** I follow up with value, not just reminders

**When my daughter called from Costa Rica:**

1. **FOR me:** This happened FOR me to prove I could handle any crisis for my children
2. **Taught me:** Love moves faster than fear. Google Translate and determination solve almost anything.
3. **Next step:** I now trust my ability to FIO in any country, any crisis. That confidence shows up in every decision.

**When I got rejected from TEDx (three times):**

1. **FOR me:** This happened FOR me to refine my message until it's undeniable
2. **Taught me:** "No" means "not yet" or "not this way," not "never"
3. **Next step:** Fourth application will incorporate everything I learned. Every rejection made the talk stronger.

This isn't about finding silver linings. It's about mining gold from experience.

The key:

# You're not just observing what happened. You're building tools for what's next.

Every FIO loop makes you smarter, stronger, better equipped for the next one. Not because you succeeded, but because you observed strategically.

Your extraction practice: After every FIO attempt, before moving on, ask these three questions. Write the answers. Writing transforms fleeting thoughts into concrete tools.

"In the middle of difficulty lies opportunity." —Albert Einstein

Another critical component in this step is sometimes missed. It's not about perfection. It's about pivoting. Let me share one of the hardest things I have had to pivot in my race directing career.

Friday, September 8th, 2023.

Twelve hours before Pumpkinman Triathlon's transition area was set to open. A week of setup behind us. Tents up. Bike racks aligned. Everything ready.

Then—boom.

A microburst storm ripped through the venue like a freight train. Seventy-plus mph winds. Lightning streaking down from the sky. Tents mangled. Transition area trashed, bike racks blown over. Port-a-potties knocked over. Debris scattered everywhere.

I had a choice: Cancel the race or figure it out.

"Okay," I said out loud. "We're going to FIO this."

At first, some were doubtful we could continue the event. I knew we didn't have a choice, we had to FIO. Cancelling wasn't an option. Everything was paid for, people had been training all year. Some had flown in all the way from the UK, Canada and across the country. I said, "Even if we have to rope off the entire tent area where we have our post-race celebration and feed people on the lawn, we will do it. If we get people to come help us set everything back up, we can make this happen."

I knew the first thing we needed to do was figure out what WAS still possible to do. There wasn't damage down at the waterfront—no trees down that could be potentially dangerous to athletes. Check—we still had a swim.

Next we needed to see what the roads were like—so the amazing people at our local bike shop who are the bike sponsors and bike course help went out to survey the damage. They could drive the run course at the same time and survey any potential damage there as well. We kept in touch with them as we were FIO'ing at the venue. We received news back that the bike course was littered with trees, down branches and live wires. I knew right then in my gut we had to cancel the bike. But I needed to see for myself before making that final decision. We hadn't gone twenty feet off the property and onto the bike course before I knew—it was unrideable. Trees down. Branches everywhere. No safe way for 500+ athletes to ride through it.

The hardest decision I've ever made: Cancel the bike portion. Convert the triathlon to a modified event with just the swim and the run.

It was a strange feeling. Having absolute decisiveness on what we needed to do to keep everyone safe, while at the same time having empathy for the athletes who trained all year for this finish line. Some wouldn't understand. But safety is non-negotiable. It's the number one priority in this industry.

Observe: Course unsafe. Venue damaged. Less than twelve hours to completely restructure.

Optimize: Swim → Run up the hill (that's your bike substitute) → Final run. Not perfect. But possible.

Celebrate: We're still having this race. These athletes still get their day.

Then the magic happened. Our community rallied.

With one social media post and a few texts, friends, neighbors and the Pumpkinman crew raced into action. They volunteered to help get this event venue back up and running. Some came with backpack leaf blowers knowing how much would need to be cleared on the venue. The tent company showed up—on a

Friday night—to repair damage. They were onsite before the storm had even passed. They literally brought a new tent, and fixed the other one that was still standing, but blown half down. Port-a-potties were being picked back up and cleaned by the company within hours. Volunteers arrived with gloves and headlamps asking "What can I do?"

Everywhere I looked, people were figuring it out. Not because they had to, but because they understood what this event meant to our community and they believed in what we were doing.

We rebuilt everything in hours. True example of community in action.

The next morning while standing in front of all of the athletes, giving the pre-race meeting information, I was staring in awe at the record number of people who, despite the storm and changes to the actual event, showed up.

Not because people were willing to race despite the changes. Because they wanted to be part of something that didn't fold when things got hard. They believed in what we do and come back year after year for their favorite race of the season.

The Pivot Lessons:

- You can't control the storm, but you can control your standards - Safety first, always
- Relationships are infrastructure - That tent company came back because of years of partnership
- Communication matters - Honest updates kept people with us
- Community is stronger than crisis - People with leaf blowers cleaning in the dark? That's love

- Pivoting isn't failing - It's responding intelligently to new data

Was it messy? Yes. Stressful? Beyond words. Did we please everyone? Of course not.

But we stood tall. We did the hard thing. We created a race day people will never forget.

That microburst taught me: Pivoting is pivotal. Life rarely goes to plan. The winners aren't those with perfect conditions. They're those who pivot fastest when conditions change.

**Now looking back at that microburst through the three questions:**

**1. How did this happen FOR me?** This storm happened FOR me to discover something I never could have learned in perfect conditions: Our community isn't just people who show up for races—they're people who show up with leaf blowers in the dark. It happened FOR me to learn that my team, my vendors, my volunteers—they're not just support, they're family. And it happened FOR me to prove that standards matter more than conditions.

**2. What did it teach me?** It taught me that pivoting isn't failing—it's intelligence in action. That people don't need perfect events; they need authentic ones. That when you're transparent about challenges, people don't abandon you—they rally. Most importantly, it taught me that "Plan B" can become legendary when executed with full commitment.

**3. How will I use this in my next step?** Now every event has what I call a "microburst protocol"—not to prevent disasters, but to transform them when they happen. I plan for chaos, not perfection. I communicate problems immediately and honestly. I trust my community to be part of the solution. And when things go sideways (because they will), I ask "How can this become part of the story?" instead of "How can I hide this?"

That storm didn't just test our event—it revealed our character. And that's the real gold in every "Well, That Happened" moment. It shows you who you really are, who your people really are, and what you're actually capable of when perfect isn't an option.

The athletes who showed up that morning didn't just get a modified race. They got to be part of a legend. Years later, people still talk about "the year of the microburst" with pride, not disappointment. They wear those medals differently. They earned them differently.

That's what happens when you observe strategically, optimize courageously, and celebrate collectively. You don't just survive the storm—you become the story everyone tells about what's possible when people FIO together.

## The Neuroscience of Why Celebration Matters

Research shows that celebrating immediately after taking action—regardless of outcome—creates a dopamine response that makes your brain want to repeat the behavior.

This is why Sara Blakely's dad was genius. By celebrating failures, he was literally rewiring his kids' brains to seek more attempts.

No celebration = no dopamine = no desire to try again.
Celebration = dopamine = brain craving more action.

### The Celebration Menu:

Micro (2-10 seconds):

- Fist pump
- Say "YES!" out loud
- Victory dance
- Text yourself

Medium (30 seconds - 2 minutes):

- Tell someone "I did it!"
- Write it in your phone notes
- Take a victory lap
- Post about the attempt (not the outcome)

Major (5+ minutes):

- Call your FIO friend
- Document the whole story
- Treat yourself
- Share with your community

## What Happens When You Skip This Step

Without Observe, Optimize & Celebrate, three things die:

1. Learning Stops You miss the lesson. Make the same mistakes. Never improve.

2. Resilience Crumbles Each setback becomes proof you "can't" instead of data you can use.

3. Motivation Disappears No dopamine reward means your brain actively avoids trying again.

I see it constantly: Someone tries once, doesn't get perfect results, quits forever. They never observed the partial wins, never optimized their approach, never celebrated their courage.

The abandonment happens here, at step three. This is why mastering this step is essential.

### Your Turn: The O-O-C Protocol

Think of something you tried recently that "didn't work."

Run it through the protocol:

OBSERVE: What actually happened? (Just facts, no drama)

OPTIMIZE: What would you do differently? (One specific change)

CELEBRATE: What took courage? (Acknowledge it out loud)

Then identify your next action based on this data.

"Celebrate what you want to see more of." —Tom Peters

## CHAPTER 6 TAKEAWAYS

- Failure is simply data, not disaster. Ask "What did you fail at?" not "What did you achieve?"
- The outcome isn't the point—what you do with it is everything
- Three outcome types: Heck Yeah, Mixed Bag, Well That Happened— they each contain gold
- The O-O-C Method: Observe (facts only), Optimize (one adjustment), Celebrate (always)
- Ask three questions: How did this happen FOR me? What did it teach me? How will I use it?
- Pivoting is pivotal—winners pivot fastest when plans go astray
- Your brain needs celebration to create dopamine and repeat the behavior
- Standards matter more than conditions—control what you can control
- Skipping this step causes learning to vanish, resilience to crumble, motivation to die
- Every outcome is useful when properly observed, optimized, and celebrated

---

## YOUR FIO ACTION STEP

Right now, before you turn the page: Think of your last 'failure' and run it through O-O-C. Write what you learned in the margin. Decide your next action. Fist pump for doing this. (Seriously. Dopamine matters.)

## The Bridge to Mastery

Remember: That microburst didn't stop us. That rain didn't cancel us. Your setback won't stop you either—if you choose to observe it, optimize from it, and celebrate that you were in the arena.

The loop only works when you complete it. All three steps. Every time.

Even when—and especially when—the storm hits.

And here's the best part: After enough loops, something magical happens. You stop thinking about the steps and start becoming someone who automatically FIOs.

The loop transforms: It stops being something you **do** and becomes something you **are.**

You'll know you've arrived when someone asks you, "How did you handle that crisis so calmly?" and you genuinely don't understand the question. Because to you, it wasn't a crisis. It was just Tuesday. Just another opportunity to figure something out.

In the next chapter, I'll show you what life looks like when FIO becomes your default operating system. When you don't have to remember to Face the Fear because you automatically face it. When you don't have to force yourself to Identify One Action because action is just what you do. When you don't have to remind yourself to Observe, Optimize and Celebrate because it's as natural as breathing.

Welcome to the FIO Life—where "figuring it out" isn't a strategy anymore.

It's just who you've become.

Turn the page. Let me show you what mastery looks like.

# Part III

# Activate

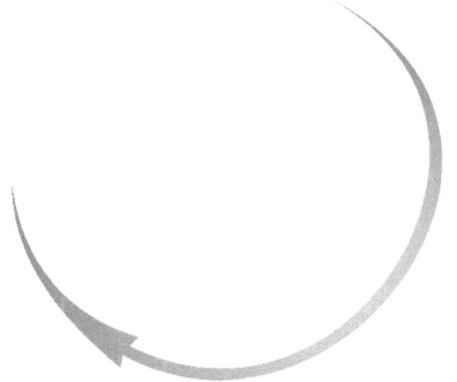

# 7

# LIVING THE FIO LIFE

When Figuring It Out Becomes Who

You Are

## The Day I Didn't Notice I Was FIO'ing

Ten hours.

That's how long I stood at the quarter-mile mark of RUNNINGMAN™ 2023, cheering for every single person who passed.

Ten. Hours.

In this chapter, I want to show you what happens when you no longer have to think about using the FIO Loop, because it has become automatic. When "figuring it out" stops being a tool and starts becoming your identity.

Back to the story. It was RUNNINGMAN™ 2023, Jesse Itzler's signature event where slightly unhinged humans run a one-mile loop for eight-hours straight. The same mile, the same direction. hour after hour for as long as they want to. The All Day Running Co. motto—"All In, All Day" becomes who you are.

I was Race Director for the race portion of RUNNINGMAN™. My job: Get everyone started, manage logistics, liaison to the timing company. All the things associated with being a Race Director. Once the race started, I was technically done on the loop.

Feeling accomplished, I decided to cheer for a few minutes. Keep energy up for the runners during those early miles.

"Power Ponytail, looking strong!"

"Red Thunder, crushing it!"

"Captain Comeback, nice form!"

Five minutes, maybe ten, then back to operations elsewhere on the grounds wherever I might be needed.

But around 15 minutes into this cheer session, a runner passed and shouted; "I only get to see you 12 more times!"

Another: "Your high-five is my fuel!"

Someone else: "Don't leave! You're part of my loops now!"

## I'd accidentally become essential to their experience.

My brain didn't debate. Didn't weigh pros and cons. It just defaulted to my core programming: "How you do anything is how you do everything."

So I stayed.

Hour 5: Runners bringing me pickle juice.

Hour 7: Voice gone, cheering with claps and presence. Hour 10: Still there for the final runner's final loop.

Ten hours later, I was still standing, still cheering, and all without it being part of the plan. Cheering on all the athletes running and walking. Some running a 5k, others running 100 miles. Whatever the distance, they each needed encouragement.

But here's what I didn't realize until weeks later, journaling about the event: I'd been living the FIO Loop for ten straight hours without a single conscious thought.

- No conscious Face the Fear (though my legs screamed to leave at hour 4)
- No deliberate Identify One Action (just stayed one more loop, then another)
- No planned Observe & Optimize (just adjusted my cheers as needed)

The loop wasn't something I made a conscious choice to do, it was something I was being.

That's when you know you've arrived—when FIO isn't a tool you use but who you are.

The goal isn't to master the FIO Loop.

The goal is to *become it.*

### The Four Stages of FIO Mastery

### Stage 1: Learning It

You consciously work each step. Face the Fear takes effort. Identifying action requires thought. Celebrating feels forced. But you do it all because you want to change.

### Stage 2: Practicing It

The steps become familiar. You recognize fear faster, you flip it quicker. Actions become easier. Celebration becomes natural. You're building new neural highways.

### Stage 3: Living It

You don't think about FIO anymore, it's just a part of who you are. Someone watching would see the pattern clearly, but you're just being yourself. The best version of you- made possible by working through hundreds of loops.

### Stage 4: Recognizing It (The Mastery Moment)

You look back and realize you've been FIO'ing without conscious thought. Like me at RUNNINGMAN™, like you will be six months from now if you start right now.

## The Compound Effect No One Talks About

That 2-hour-53-minute video to Jesse Itzler? It wasn't one opportunity. It was the first domino.

Volunteering at Driveway to Hell led to →

Producing Hell on the Hill Maine led to →

Race Director at Runningman led to →

Three years of partnership led to →

This book in your hands.

One FIO action isn't equal to one result. Each FIO action created an ecosystem of possibility.

Your first FIO won't just solve your immediate problem. It will:

- Build evidence you're capable
- Attract other FIO'ers to you
- Create opportunities you can't yet imagine
- Transform you into a completely different life

But only if you take that first action.

**The Two Versions of Your Future**

Let me show you two lives. Both possible. You choose which one becomes real.

**VERSION 1: The Waiting Life (Path 1 or 2 Forever)**

Five years from now, you have the same dreams. But they're quieter now. Covered in dust.

You still talk about what you're "going to do." Your friends nod politely—they've heard this before.

You watch people—people no smarter, no luckier—living your dreams. You tell yourself they had advantages. Better timing. More support.

The gap between your real life and phantom life has become a canyon. Crossing feels impossible now.

At night, sometimes, you remember reading this book. Remember feeling like change was possible. You wonder what would have happened if you'd actually done something about it.

## VERSION 2: The FIO Life (Path 3 From Today Forward)

Five years from now, your life is unrecognizable.

Not because you won the lottery or discovered you had secret talents. But because you took one action. Then another. Then another.

That business you dreamed about? It exists. That conversation you avoided? It healed everything. That race you thought impossible? There's a medal on your wall. That person you wanted to become? You see them in the mirror.

People ask how you did it. You smile: "I just figured it out."

You remember reading this book. Remember the moment you decided to stop waiting. That moment becomes the line you draw—before FIO and after FIO.

Everything good in your life traces back to that one decision.

## Your FIO Identity (This Is Who You Are Now)

Read this out loud. Yes, really. Even if people are around. Especially if people are around.

**I am someone who figures things out.**

I don't wait for perfection. I start with what I have.

I don't need all the answers. I need one next action.

I don't avoid fear lines. I cross them.

I don't let outcomes define me. I let them teach me.

I am not my fear. I am my action despite fear.

I am not my failures. I am my willingness to try.

I am not waiting for someday. I am living in today.

**I am a FIO'er.**

This is who I am. This is what I do. I figure it out.

## Building Your FIO Tribe

"You become the average of the five people you spend the most time with." — Jim Rohn

Look at your five. Are they FIO'ers or are they "someday-itis" sufferers?

When I started hanging around Jesse Itzler's crew, everything accelerated. Not because they taught me anything. Because FIO was just their normal.

## The FIO Five Audit

Write the names of your five tribe:

1. _____ (FIO or "someday-itis"?)
2. _____ (FIO or "someday-itis"?)
3. _____ (FIO or "someday-itis"?)
4. _____ (FIO or "someday-itis"?)
5. _____ (FIO or "someday-itis"?)

You don't have to dump your "someday-itis" friends. But add some FIO'ers. Find them at starting lines, doing scary things, building without permission.

When you become someone who FIOs, you attract others who FIO. Your five changes. Your normal changes. Your life changes.

### The RUNNINGMAN™ Revelation

My son Ethan was working at the aid station at RUNNINGMAN™ that first year when I cheered for 10 hours. His job? Keep runners fueled and hydrated.

But watching loop after loop, the energy inspired him.

"Mom, I'm going to run a few loops on my break."

A few became a marathon. His first ever. ALL WHILE WORKING THE AID STATION.

Running loops, emptying trash, running more loops, restocking water. At one point, carrying a trash bag for a quarter mile mid-run.

Twenty-six-point-two miles. Figured out in real-time.

That's what happens in FIO environments—it becomes contagious. My son caught it from me. You'll pass it to someone else. This is how movements start.

Fast forward to RUNNINGMAN™ 2025. I'm back, this time for eight hours straight in Sara Blakely's SNEEX™—those genius stiletto sneakers she created to help women stand all day without pain. On that same grass one-mile loop. A runner stumbled past, walking now, that familiar "I can't do this" look in his eyes.

"FIGURE IT OUT!" I yelled. "Just take the next step—that's all you need!"

He looked at me like I was insane. Then he started running again.

Eight hours. Hundreds of runners. Each one getting reminded that they can figure out one more loop, one more mile, one more step. My feet never hurt—Sara had FIO'd that problem. My voice never quit—Jesse had FIO'd an event that creates that endless energy.

From Ethan catching the FIO spirit year one to me passing it on to strangers—this is how it spreads. In SNEEX™ from Sara Blakely who started SPANX® with $5,000, at Jesse Itzler's event he created from pure vision, cheering people who are FIO'ing their own impossible.

None of us belong here on paper. All of us belong here in practice.

## Your Stories Are Waiting

When I'm 90 in my rocking chair, here's what I'll remember:

Not the perfect moments. The messy ones. Not when I felt ready. When I acted despite terror. Not smooth successes. The disasters I turned into data.

The 2 AM courage at RAAM. The midnight Facebook post creating Rick's Run. The ski helmet Zoom with Jesse. The infamous microburst that could have stopped Pumpkinman. But I did not let it.

These stories exist because I crossed fear lines.

What stories will you remember? The time you almost? Or the time you did?

Your stories are waiting on the other side of fear. But they only become real when you cross.

## The Next 24 Hours (This Matters More Than Everything Else)

Right now, before you close this book:

**My next fear line is:** _____

**In the next 24 hours, I will:** _____

Take out your phone. Set a reminder for exactly 24 hours from now. Title it: "DID YOU FIO?"

When that reminder goes off, you'll either be celebrating or explaining to yourself why you're still waiting.

Which conversation do you want to have with yourself tomorrow?

## The Rocking Chair Test

Close your eyes. Picture yourself at 90, in that rocking chair, looking back at today.

That version of you isn't saying "I'm glad you waited." They're not saying "Good thing you played it safe."

They're saying: "Thank you for being brave." "Thank you for not letting fear win." "Thank you for giving me stories worth telling." "Thank you for figuring it out."

That future you is counting on present you to make decisions they'll be proud of.

Don't let them down.

**This Is Your Moment**

You have two choices right now:

1. Close this book and go back to waiting. Add it to the pile of "good ideas" you never acted on.
2. Close this book and immediately take ONE action. Become living proof that FIO works.

18 years ago, I chose option 2 and crossed the Boston Marathon finish line with no real plan.

Today, it's your turn.

The loop is simple: Face it. Identify action. Take it. Learn from it.

But simple isn't easy. That's why most people stay stuck.

You're not most people anymore.

You're someone who figures things out.

Prove it.

**Turn the page. Then make it real.**

Three years from now, you'll be one of three people:

Still stuck.

Still preparing.

Or fully FIO'ing.

# 8

# Your FIO Moment

"I just decided to FIO." —Every person who ever changed their life

## You're Not the Same Person Who Started This Book

Something shifted while you were reading.

It was subtle. Happened somewhere between learning about the three paths and practicing the loop. Maybe it was when you recognized yourself in my stories. Maybe it was when you thought "I could do that" for the fifth time.

That person who picked up this book wondering if they could change? Gone.

You're someone different now. Someone who knows—not believes, not hopes, but KNOWS—you can figure things out.

But knowing and doing are different animals. This chapter is the bridge between them.

## The Next 24 Hours Matter More Than the Next 24 Years

Every transformation has a moment. A line. A before and after.

This is yours.

The person who started this book had excuses. Had "someday." Had "when I'm ready."

You don't have those anymore. You have knowledge. You have tools. You have evidence from my life and the lives of thousands of others that FIO works.

Now you need one more thing: Your own evidence.

## The Truth Nobody Wants to Hear

You already know what you need to do. It's the thing that popped into your head in Chapter 1 and hasn't left. The thing you thought about during every story I told. The thing that made your stomach tighten when I talked about fear lines.

You don't need more information. You don't need more preparation. You don't need more time.

You need to take one action in the next 24 hours.

Not because I'm telling you to. Because your 90-year-old self is begging you to.

## Your 90-Year-Old Self Is Watching

Actually, two versions of your 90-year-old self are watching.

**Version One:** The one who acted in the next 24 hours. They're laughing, telling the story of how scared they were, how unprepared, how they did it anyway. Their eyes light up remembering. They lean forward saying, "Let me tell you about the time I had no idea what I was doing but..." They have proof they lived.

**Version Two:** The one who waited. They're quiet. When asked about their dreams, they say "timing wasn't right." When asked about risks, they say "I played it safe." When asked about their story, they have explanations instead of experiences.

Remember what I told you in the beginning? Regret is born between two lives—the life you're living and the life you wish you were living.

Version Two is trapped there forever. They spent decades thinking about what they wanted to do instead of doing it. They lived a parallel existence of "I wish I had" running alongside "I never did."

Version One has no parallel life. They don't wonder "what if" because they know what happened. They tried. They figured it out. They have one life, fully lived.

Right now, both versions exist as possibilities.

In 24 hours, you choose which one becomes real.

Your 90-year-old self isn't just watching—they're holding their breath, waiting to see if they get to exist as someone who lived fully or someone who lived with constant wondering.

The space between who you are and who you want to be? It closes or widens based on what you do next.

Don't sentence them to a lifetime of wondering.

Don't let them become the person who always wished they'd tried.

Choose Version One. Choose the stories. Choose the life actually lived.

Choose to FIO.

## The Ripple You're About to Start

When you take action in the next 24 hours, something beautiful happens. Not just for you—for everyone around you.

Your courage becomes contagious. People who've been watching you, waiting to see if change is really possible, suddenly get permission to try. Your kids learn that adults don't just dream— they do. Your friends see that waiting isn't mandatory. Your colleagues catch your energy and start their own loops.

You become living proof that regular people can figure things out.

But here's the real magic: You become proof to yourself. And once you have that proof, that evidence that you're someone who takes action despite fear, everything changes.

## Your FIO Moment

I'm not going to give you a complex pledge or a long list of promises to make. You need simplicity, not complexity. You need one clear action, not ten good intentions.

Think about your fear line—the one that's been with you this entire book. The thing you've been avoiding, postponing, overthinking.

Got it? Good.

Now, what's ONE action you could take toward it in the next 24 hours? Not the perfect action. Not the complete solution. Just one step that moves you from thinking to doing.

Write it down. Right here, right now:

**My fear line:** _____

**My ONE action in the next 24 hours:**

_____

**When I'll do it:** _____

Now set a reminder on your phone for exactly 24 hours from now. Title it: "Did I FIO?"

When it goes off tomorrow, you'll know if you kept your promise to yourself.

## The Stories Waiting for You

Eighteen years ago, I stood at the Boston Marathon starting line with lingering bronchitis and no business being there. If someone had told me that one decision would lead to directing races, raising money for veterans, writing a book, and changing thousands of lives, I would have thought they were insane.

But that's how FIO works. One action creates more ripples than you can imagine.

The email you're about to send might lead to a partnership that changes your career. The conversation you're about to have might heal a relationship you thought was lost. The application you're about to submit might open doors you didn't know existed. The class you're about to sign up for might introduce you to your next chapter.

Or it might not. And that's okay too. Because even if that specific action doesn't lead where you expect, it leads to the next action, and the next, and the next. It builds your FIO muscle. It creates evidence. It starts momentum.

Your stories—the ones you'll tell at 90—they're waiting on the other side of the next 24 hours.

## This Is Not the End

Books end, but transformations don't. This is not a conclusion—**it's a beginning.**

You came looking for a way to stop waiting and start moving. You found it. The FIO Loop isn't just something you've read about—it's something you're about to live.

Here's what I know after twenty-two years of FIO'ing: **Decisions create action.** Not planning. Not preparing. Not thinking. Decisions.

The moment you decide—truly decide—to send that email, have that conversation, start that project, the action follows. The decision is the hard part. The action? That's just following through on what you've already committed to in your mind.

Tomorrow, when that reminder goes off, you'll either celebrate that you took action or you'll understand what stopped you so you can try again. Either way, you're learning. Either way, you're closer to who you are becoming.

And once you complete that first loop—once you face that fear, take that action, and observe what happens—you'll want to do it again. And again. And again.

Until one day, someone will ask you, "How did you build this life? How did you become this person? How did you figure it all out?"

And you'll smile, remembering this moment, and say:

"I just decided to FIO."

# YOUR FIO QUICK REFERENCE GUIDE

## GET FREE ACCESS TO THE 6-WEEK FIO EXPERIENCE

This book is designed to be used — not just read.

When you purchase The FIO Mindset, you'll receive free access to the 6-Week FIO Experience, a guided, step-by-step work-through designed to help you apply the mindset in real life.

The experience will be run live and then made available on-demand, so you can move through it at your own pace.

Scan the QR code below to get started.

thefiomindset.com

# THE FIO LOOP™ AT A GLANCE

**STEP 1: FACE THE FEAR & FLIP IT** Name it → Claim it → Flip it

**STEP 2: IDENTIFY ONE ACTION** One thing. Tiny. Today.

**STEP 3: OBSERVE, OPTIMIZE & CELEBRATE** What happened? What did I learn? What's next?

---

# THE THREE PATHS DIAGNOSTIC

Which path are you on right now?

□ **PATH 1:** "I can't" (Stuck forever) □ **PATH 2:** "I need to prepare more" (Stuck preparing)
□ **PATH 3:** "I'll figure it out" (Already moving)

**To jump to Path 3:** Take one action in the next hour

---

# THE DAILY FIO CHECK

Every night, ask yourself:

- Did I face a fear today? □
- Did I take one action? □
- Did I celebrate trying? □
- What did I learn? _____
- What's tomorrow's ONE action? _____

---

# EMERGENCY FIO PROTOCOL

*When panic/paralysis hits*

1. **BREATHE:** 4 counts in, 6 counts out
2. **SHRINK:** What's the tiniest possible step?
3. **MOVE:** Do that tiny thing in next 10 minutes
4. **CELEBRATE:** You're in motion
5. **REPEAT:** Next tiny step appears

# THE 30-DAY FIO CHALLENGE

**Your commitment:** Complete one FIO Loop every day for 30 days

Track your progress at thefiomindset.com/challenge or use this simple tracker:

**Week 1:** ☐ ☐ ☐ ☐ ☐ ☐ ☐

**Week 2:** ☐ ☐ ☐ ☐ ☐ ☐ ☐

**Week 3:** ☐ ☐ ☐ ☐ ☐ ☐ ☐

**Week 4:** ☐ ☐ ☐ ☐ ☐ ☐ ☐ **Bonus Days:** ☐ ☐

**Day 10 Check-in:** I'm someone who _____

**Day 20 Check-in:** I'm someone who _____

**Day 30 Celebration:** I'm someone who _____

---

# YOUR FIO ACCOUNTABILITY SYSTEM

**Option 1: Find Your FIO Partner** Text this to someone today: "I'm doing the FIO Challenge from The FIO Mindset. Will you check in with me weekly to see if I'm taking action? I'll do the same for you."

**Option 2: Join the FIO Community** Connect with the community at www.thefiomindset.com

# SHARE YOUR FIO STORY

When you complete your first FIO Loop, share it:

**Instagram/Social:** @thefiomindset @rachelmartinmaine

# YOUR FIRST FIO STARTS NOW

Before you close this book:

1. Name your fear: _____
2. Choose ONE tiny action: _____
3. When will you do it? _____
4. Set a phone alarm now
5. Come back and check: □ I DID IT!

**Remember:** You don't need the whole toolkit. You just need to start with one tool, one action, one FIO.

# KEEP THE FIO MOMENTUM GOING

**Free Resources:** thefiomindset.com

The gap between your current life and your dream life is one FIO Loop.

**Start now.**

## AUTHOR'S NOTE

Creating Ripples from Every FIO:

This book taught me something powerful: When you FIO your own life, you create ripples that extend far beyond yourself. That's why I'm committed to making sure this book creates literal ripples of change.

A portion of every single sale of The FIO Mindset supports three organizations that are dear to my heart:

**LOCALLY**: The Marshwood Education Foundation provides grants to teachers for innovative ideas that fall outside the regular school budget. I have been on this since its inception and am so proud of the work we do.

**NATIONALLY:** The Common Ground Sister City Project connects South Berwick, Maine with Tuskegee, Alabama, building bridges across divides and proving that different communities can find common ground. One of my favorite projects I have ever been a part of.

**GLOBALLY:** Village Impact is my friend's non-profit that builds schools in rural Kenya, giving children the education that changes not just their lives, but entire communities.

Why these three? Because I believe in the compound effect of action. One person taking action in their community. Communities connecting across the country. And extending that impact across the globe. Local to global, one FIO at a time.

If this book helped you cross a fear line, know that your purchase is helping a student in Maine get new opportunities, communities in Alabama and Maine build understanding, and children in Kenya getting an education.

That's the ultimate FIO Loop—your transformation creating transformation for others.

Want to deepen the impact? Visit TheFIOMindset.com/impact to learn more about these organizations or make an additional donation.

Together, we're not just figuring it out. We're helping others figure it out too. Let's FIO—locally, nationally, and globally.

With gratitude and determination, Rachel

# COMPLETE REFERENCES AND ACKNOWLEDGMENTS

*For The FIO Mindset by Rachel Martin*

## QUOTES AND CITATIONS

The following quotes and concepts have been used with attribution throughout this book:

**Aristotle.** "We are what we repeatedly do. Excellence, then, is not an act, but a habit."

**Blakely, Sara.** References to Sara Blakely's father's weekly question "What did you fail at this week?" are based on widely reported interviews and her public speeches about her upbringing and the founding of SPANX®.

**Campbell, Joseph.** "The cave you fear to enter holds the treasure you seek."

**Canfield, Jack.** "Everything you want is on the other side of fear."

**da Vinci, Leonardo.** "I have been impressed with the urgency of doing. Knowing is not enough; we must apply. Being willing is not enough; we must do."

**Dillard, Annie.** "How we spend our days is, of course, how we spend our lives."

**Disney, Walt.** "The way to get started is to quit talking and begin doing."

**Dweck, Carol S.** *Mindset: The New Psychology of Success.* New York: Random House, 2006. References to growth mindset research and framework are based on Dr. Dweck's groundbreaking work. Readers are encouraged to read her book for a deeper understanding of the growth mindset foundation.

**Einstein, Albert.** "In the middle of difficulty lies opportunity."

**Ford, Henry.** "Whether you think you can, or you think you can't—you're right."

**Jung, Carl.** "Until you make the unconscious conscious, it will direct your life and you will call it fate."

**Mandela, Nelson.** "I learned that courage was not the absence of fear, but the triumph over it."

**Maslow, Abraham.** "In any given moment we have two options: to step forward into growth or step back into safety."

**Peters, Tom.** "Celebrate what you want to see more of."

**Robbins, Tony.** "Never leave the site of a goal without taking action toward it." From personal development programs and goal-setting workshops.

**Roosevelt, Eleanor.** "Do one thing every day that scares you."

**Roosevelt, Theodore.** "In any moment of decision, the best thing you can do is the right thing, the next best thing is the wrong thing, and the worst thing you can do is nothing."

**Rohn, Jim.** "Stand guard at the door of your mind."

**Schuller, Robert.** "What would you attempt to do if you knew you could not fail?"

**Winfrey, Oprah.** "The more you praise and celebrate your life, the more there is in life to celebrate."

# RESEARCH AND SCIENCE

### Brain Development and Childhood Beliefs:

- References to beliefs formed by age seven based on critical period research in developmental psychology
- Bowlby, John. *Attachment and Loss* (1969-1980)
- Piaget, Jean. *The Psychology of the Child* (1969)

### Evolutionary Psychology and Survival Mechanisms:

- "Your brain wasn't designed for happiness—it was designed for survival" based on:
- Cosmides, L. & Tooby, J. *The Adapted Mind: Evolutionary Psychology and the Generation of Culture* (1992)
- MacLean, Paul. *The Triune Brain in Evolution* (1990)

### Fear and the Amygdala:

- References to amygdala activation and fear response based on:
- LeDoux, Joseph. *The Emotional Brain: The Mysterious Underpinnings of Emotional Life* (1996)
- Phelps, E. A. (2006). "Emotion and cognition: Insights from studies of the human amygdala." *Annual Review of Psychology*

### Stress Hormones and Response:

- References to cortisol and adrenaline based on:
- Sapolsky, Robert. *Why Zebras Don't Get Ulcers* (2004)
- McEwen, B. S. (2007). "Physiology and neurobiology of stress and adaptation." *Physiological Reviews*

### Prefrontal Cortex and Decision-Making:

- Arnsten, A. F. (2009). "Stress signalling pathways that impair prefrontal cortex structure and function." *Nature Reviews Neuroscience*

### Dopamine and Celebration:

- References to dopamine response and reward systems based on:
- Schultz, W. (2015). "Neuronal reward and decision signals." *Neuron*
- Wise, R. A. (2004). "Dopamine, learning and motivation." *Nature Reviews Neuroscience*
- Berridge, K. C. & Robinson, T. E. (1998). "What is the role of dopamine in reward?" *Brain Research Reviews*

### Neuroplasticity:

- "Your brain literally rewires based on evidence" based on:
- Doidge, Norman. *The Brain That Changes Itself* (2007)
- Pascual-Leone, A. et al. (2005). "The plastic human brain cortex." *Annual Review of Neuroscience*
- Draganski, B. et al. (2004). "Neuroplasticity: Changes in grey matter induced by training." *Nature*

### Habit Formation:

- References to habit loops and automatic behavior based on:
- Duhigg, Charles. *The Power of Habit* (2012)
- Clear, James. *Atomic Habits* (2018)
- Wood, W., & Neal, D. T. (2007). "A new look at habits and the habit-goal interface." *Psychological Review*
- Fogg, BJ. *Tiny Habits: The Small Changes That Change Everything* (2019)

## Confidence and Self-Efficacy:

- "Confidence is a byproduct, not a prerequisite" based on:
- Bandura, Albert. *Self-Efficacy: The Exercise of Control* (1997)

## Cognitive Reframing:

- References to changing thoughts to change outcomes based on:
- Beck, Aaron T. *Cognitive Therapy and the Emotional Disorders* (1976)

- Beck, J. S. *Cognitive Behavior Therapy: Basics and Beyond* (2011)
- Ellis, Albert. *Reason and Emotion in Psychotherapy* (1962)

## Optimism Research:

- References to explanatory style and optimism based on:
- Seligman, Martin E.P. *Learned Optimism* (1991)
- Peterson, C., & Seligman, M. E. (2004). *Character Strengths and Virtues*

## Growth Mindset:

- Dweck, Carol S. *Mindset: The New Psychology of Success.* New York: Random House, 2006
- Dweck, C.S. & Yeager, D.S. (2019). "Mindsets: A view from two eras."
- Perspectives on Psychological Science  The terms "fixed mindset" and "growth mindset" are used in this book under fair educational use and do not reproduce any proprietary diagrams, charts, or materials from Dr. Dweck's work.

**Note:** Neuroscience and psychology concepts have been simplified for general readership. While based on peer-reviewed research, the practical applications are the author's interpretation and should not replace professional psychological or medical advice. Neuroscience explanations in this book are simplified

for general readership and are not intended as clinical, diagnostic, or medical guidance.

# CONTENT NOTES

**The FIO Loop™** is the proprietary framework created by Rachel Martin based on twenty-two years of experience in endurance sports, race directing, and personal development.

**Launching Beliefs™** is an original concept developed by Rachel Martin to describe the commitment to figure things out rather than the confidence that you already know how.

All personal stories and anecdotes are from the author's direct experience unless otherwise noted. Names have been used with permission where applicable.

References to Race Across America (RAAM) are based on the author's personal experience crewing for the event from 2021-2023.

The Pumpkinman Triathlon microburst incident occurred on September 8, 2023, and is documented through event records and participant accounts.

Rick's Run, founded in 2016, is an annual Memorial Day charity race benefiting local veterans. To date, it has raised tens of thousands of dollars for veteran causes.

The Common Ground Sister City Project between South Berwick, Maine and Tuskegee, Alabama began in 2017 and continues as of time of this publication.

# PERMISSIONS AND ACKNOWLEDGMENTS

Jesse Itzler's story is shared with awareness of public information about his career and ventures. The author's personal interaction with Mr. Itzler is described from her own perspective.

Pat McGee's participation in private events is shared with respect for his privacy and professional reputation.

All social media handles and hashtags (@thefiomindset, #MyFIOMoment) are property of Rachel Martin and Forward Motion Events.

# A NOTE ON ATTRIBUTION

Every effort has been made to trace the ownership of copyrighted material and to make due acknowledgment. If any omission has been made or error occurred, please notify the publisher for correction in future editions.

Some quotes commonly attributed to certain sources may have disputed or unclear origins. Where attribution is uncertain, the most commonly accepted source has been used.

# TRADEMARK ACKNOWLEDGMENTS

The FIO Loop™, The FIO Mindset™, and Launching Beliefs™ are trademarks of Rachel Martin.

SPANX® is a registered trademark of SPANX, Inc.

All other trademarks mentioned in this book are the property of their respective owners.

# CONTACT

Share your FIO story: www.thefiomindset.com

Email: thefiomindset@gmail.com

Instagram: @thefiomindset @rachelmartinmaine

---

www.ingramcontent.com/pod-product-compliance
Lightning Source LLC
Chambersburg PA
CBHW021236130626
46554CB00004B/1512